Overcoming Deceit: Expository on the World of Lies and Illusions

Overcoming Deceit: Expository on the World of Lies and Illusions

Copyright © 2023 Bimpe Gold-Idowu.

First Edition 2022 Bimpe Gold-Idowu

All rights reserved. No part of this book may be reproduced or transmitted in any form or by any means without the written permission from the author or publisher, except in the case of brief quotations embodied in critical reviews and certain other non-commercial uses permitted by copyright law.

Published by Seed Publishing House

Overcoming Deceit: Expository on the World of Lies and Illusions

BIMPE GOLD-IDOWU

Books by Bimpe Gold-Idowu

Non-Fiction

Arts of Miracle

Overcoming Deceit: Expository on the World of Lies and Illusions

Fiction

The Girl from the Sea (Richie and the Mermaid Princess Series 1)

When Love Comes Calling: The Ultimate Love

The Adamites: Protector of the Universe Series 1

DEDICATION

I dedicate this book to God The Father, Son and Holy Spirit for His grace upon me to be in His vineyard. Also to my life partner, prayer partner, best friend, husband, Idowu Olaniyi Ezekiel for his support, patience and love, your anointing will never run dry in Jesus Christ's name. Amen. I love you, darling Diamond.

Overcoming Deceit: Expository on the World of Lies and Illusions

All Scripture references are taken from the Holy Bible:
King James Version KJV
King James Version American KJVA
American Standard Version ASV
Amplified Bible AMP
Christian Standard Bible CSB
And references from First and Second Book of Adam and Eve

Bimpe Gold-Idowu

CONTENTS

Introduction	xi
Deceit	1
Darkness as Light	2
False Promise, Prophecy or Vision	16
Trials, Temptations and Tribulations of Satan that look like God's Chastise.	25
Alternate route offer – a Shortcut	42
Another Better Plan	56
Agreement by Compulsion	67
Hurtful Advice	80
Sexual Desire	92
Secrecy	100
Re-incarnation	109
Ungodly Fellowship	119
Emergence of Overcomer	133

Introduction

I compared unbelievers to believers in the church today. I feel sad seeing a minor difference in both. Members no more have high regards for them, unlike centuries back. It makes no difference if it is the gospel or a flowery sermon coming from the altar. It is true Satan's deception has caused many believers to alter their priorities. Satan's solution sometimes seems enticing and is faster than the usual biblical solution. It is easier to choose his faster solution than to go on a long and lonely path of righteousness, forgetting that his way only leads to doom.

I applied Adam and Eve's experiences in dealing with Satan's schemes after they left the garden in the book of Adam and Eve to the present circumstances of mankind.

It is only when believers understand forms Satan uses in manipulation men and they overcome his deception.

Overcoming Deceit is an eye opening and I hope it will lead those that have fallen from the faith back to Christ.

Job 13:35

"They conceive trouble and give birth to evil; their womb fashions deceit."

CHAPTER ONE
DARKNESS AS LIGHT

What is Deceit?

Deceit is a make believe of the devil leading to confusion. It is an imitation, a photocopy looking almost like the original, but its works can never be perfect.

Who brought Deceit?

Satan.

Genesis 3:1 KJV

"Now the serpent was more cunny than any beast of the field which the Lord God had made. And he said unto the woman, Yea, hath God said, Ye shall not eat of every tree of the garden?"

Satan exaggerated the instruction of God. He made it looked so difficult, portraying God as cruel.

Genesis 3:4-5 KJV

"And the serpent said unto the woman, Ye shall not surely die. For God doth know that in the day ye eat thereof, then your eyes shall be opened, and ye shall be as gods, knowing good and evil."

He lied to them because at that moment their eyes were opened to the world of sin and death but their spiritual eyes to the heavenly realm became blind. Devil has many forms of deceit he usually makes use of in order to get man on the wrong side of God. Let us look at these forms.

Forms of Deceit

There are many forms or ways the devil uses to carry out his deceit. He can come in form of light, man, good, bad, natural force, even he can claim to be God. All these things are with the intention of leading man away from the true God, we must not be ignorant of the devil's antics.

Darkness as Light

Satan can disguise himself to be God, demons (falling angels) can come in form of Messengers of God; calling themselves Angels of Light but in reality they are demons (angels of darkness). Lie can sound like the truth just like a fake jewelry can looks like gold.

The 1st Book Of Adam and Eve CHAP. III: 1-6.

1 GOD said to Adam, "I have ordained on this earth days and years, and thou and thy seed shall dwell and walk in it, until the days and years are fulfilled; when I shall send the Word that created thee, and against which thou hast transgressed, the Word that made thee come out of the garden and that raised thee when thou wast fallen.

2 Yea, the Word that will again save thee when the five days and a half are fulfilled."

3 But when Adam heard these words from God, and of the great five days and a half, he did not understand the meaning of them.

4 For Adam was thinking that there would be but five days and a half for him, to the end of the world.

5 And Adam wept, and prayed God to explain it to him.

6 Then God in His mercy for Adam who was made after His own image and similitude, explained to him, that these were 5,000 and 500 years; and how One would then come and save him and his seed.

After Adam and Eve came out of the garden of Eden, God placed them at the Western side of the garden in a cave called Cave of Treasure. Satan anger towards man multiples because God was still interested in man even after the fall of man, an opportunity that was not given to Satan. To crown it all, the earth Satan thought that he would dominate, thereby converting it to his own was given to man to rule over it. Satan and his hosts still refuse to lose it all thereby coming together to bring different forms of deceit to man.

The First Book Of Adam and Eve CHAP. XXVII.: 1-5

1 When Satan, the hater of all good, saw how they continued in prayer, and how God communed with them, and comforted them, and how He had accepted their offering--Satan made an apparition.

2 He began with transforming his hosts; in his hands was a flashing fire, and they were in a great light.

3 He then placed his throne near the mouth of the cave because he could not enter into it by reason of their prayers. And he shed light into the cave, until the cave glistened over Adam and Eve; while his hosts began to sing praises.

4 And Satan did this, in order that when Adam saw

the light, he should think within himself that it was a heavenly light, and that Satan's hosts were angels; and that God had sent them to watch at the cave, and to give him light in the darkness.

5 So that when Adam came out of the cave and saw them, and Adam and Eve bowed to Satan, then he would overcome Adam thereby, and a second time humble him before God.

Satan deceives man by pretending to be God by bringing his own version of vision. Demons can also disguise themselves to be Angels claiming to bring words from God. Their words always bring in uncertainty and confusion. Their words are always harsh and insensitive, building rebellion in man if not ignored or stopped in time.

The First Book Of Adam and Eve CHAP. XXVIII (28) : 1-10

1 BUT when the wily Satan saw them, that they were going to the garden, he gathered together his host, and came in appearance upon a cloud, intent on deceiving them.

2 But when Adam and Eve saw him thus in a vision, they thought they were angels of God come to comfort them about their having left the garden, or to bring them

back again into it.

3 And Adam spread his hands unto God, beseeching Him to make him understand what they were.

4 Then Satan, the hater of all good, said unto Adam, "O Adam, I am an angel of the great God; and, behold the hosts that surround me.

5 "God has sent me and them to take thee and bring thee to the border of the garden northwards; to the shore of the clear sea, and bathe thee and Eve in it, and raise you to your former gladness, that ye return again to the garden."

6 These words sank into the heart of Adam and Eve.

7 Yet God withheld His Word from Adam, and did not make him understand at once, but waited to see his strength; whether he would be overcome as Eve was when in the garden, or whether he would prevail.

8 Then Satan called to Adam and Eve, and said, "Behold, we go to the sea of water," and they began to go.

9 And Adam and Eve followed them at some little distance.

10 But when they came to the mountain to the north of the garden, a very high mountain, without any steps to the top of it, the Devil drew near to Adam and Eve, and made them go up to the top in reality, and not in a vision;

wishing, as he did, to throw them down and kill them, and to wipe off their name from the earth; so that this earth should remain to him and his hosts alone.

Satan can easily deceive human because we always expect messages that will please to us and not actually the word of truth. Adam and Eve wanted to go back to the garden even though God already told them to stay where they were until 5,500 years, when He will send the Word to bring them back.

- God's communication is always clear. An unclear vision, prophecy, or language will cause confusion. God is not an author of confusion. When he speaks to you in whatever form He may take, it is always clear.
- God is unchangeable. Once he makes a promise or covenant, He will stand by it. God won't tell you green today and tomorrow change it to white.

Numbers 23:19 KJV

"God is not a man, that he should lie; neither the son of man, that he should repent: hath he said, and shall he not do it? or hath he spoken, and shall he not make it good?"

Once He speaks, it stands. God told them to wait for 5,500 years, it must come to pass. Let us look at the case of the Prophet from Judah and the old Prophet.

1 Kings 13:14-22 KJV

"And went after the man of God, and found him sitting under an oak: and he said unto him, Art thou the man of God that camest from Judah? And he said, I am.

Then he said unto him, Come home with me, and eat bread.

And he said, I may not return with thee, nor go in with thee: neither will I eat bread nor drink water with thee in this place: For it was said to me by the word of the Lord, Thou shalt eat no bread nor drink water there, nor turn again to go by the way that thou camest.

He said unto him, I am a prophet also as thou art; and an angel spake unto me by the word of the Lord, saying, Bring him back with thee into thine house, that he may eat bread and drink water. But he lied unto him.

So he went back with him, and did eat bread in his house, and drank water. And it came to pass, as they sat at the table, that the word of the Lord came unto the prophet that brought him back:

And he cried unto the man of God that came from Judah, saying, Thus saith the Lord, Forasmuch as thou hast disobeyed the mouth of the Lord, and hast not kept the commandment which the Lord thy God commanded thee,

But camest back, and hast eaten bread and drunk water in the place, of the which the Lord did say to thee, eat no bread, and drink no water; thy carcass shall not come unto the sepulchre of thy fathers."

Message given to the prophet from Judah was clear and complete, it was to guide him but he followed man, not minding the change in tone of the message.

Overcoming Darkness and Demons.
We have no power of our own. We can only overcome Satan and his host is by the help of the Almighty Himself;

The First Book Of Adam and Eve CHAP. XXIX.(29):5-8

5 And Adam wept before the Lord God, and begged and entreated Him to give him something from the garden, as a token to him, wherein to be comforted.

6 And God looked upon Adam's thought, and sent the

angel Michael as far as the sea that reaches unto India, to take from thence golden rods and bring them to Adam.

7 This did God in His wisdom, in order that these golden rods, being with Adam in the cave, should shine forth with light in the night around him, and put an end to his fear of the darkness.

8 Then the angel Michael went down by God's order, took golden rods, as God had commanded him, and brought them to God.

CHAP. XXX.(30):1-8

1 AFTER these things, God commanded the angel Gabriel to go down to the garden, and say to the cherub who kept it, "Behold, God has commanded me to come into the garden, and to take thence sweet smelling incense, and give it to Adam."

2 Then the angel Gabriel went down by God's order to the garden, and told the cherub as God had commanded him.

3 The cherub then said, "Well." And Gabriel went in and took the incense.

4 Then God commanded His angel Raphael to go down to the garden, and speak to the cherub about some myrrh, to give to Adam.

5 And the angel Raphael went down and told the cherub as God had commanded him, and the cherub said, "Well." Then Raphael went in and took the myrrh.

6 The golden rods were from the Indian sea, where there are precious stones. The incense was from the eastern border of the garden; and the myrrh from the western border, whence bitterness came upon Adam.

7 And the angels brought these three things to God, by the Tree of Life, in the garden.

8 Then God said to the angels, "Dip them in the spring of water; then take them and sprinkle their water over Adam and Eve, that they be a little comforted in their sorrow, and give them to Adam and Eve.

- Things from the Garden - Ask for the Holy Spirit, the comforter. It is the Spirit of God that can discern good and bad.

John 16:13 KJVA

"Howbeit when he, the Spirit of truth, is come, he will guide you into all truth: for he shall not speak of himself; but whatsoever he shall hear, that shall he speak: and he will show you things to come."

Discerning Spirit is one of the gifts of the Holy Spirit. This gift is very important to a child of God so that you won't fall prey to the devil.

1st Corinthians 12:10 KJVA

"To another the working of miracles; to another prophecy; to another discerning of spirits; to another divers kinds of tongues; to another the interpretation of tongues:"

- Golden Rod – Light that shines in darkness.

Without the salvation of Jesus Christ and receiving the grace to walk in him, there can be no light without Him because Jesus Christ is the Light.

John 8:12 KJVA

"Then spake Jesus again unto them, saying, I am the light of the world: he that follow me shall not walk in darkness, but shall have the light of life."

- Incense- A Thankful Heart. (Psalms 51:10,12)

Psalm 51:10-12 KJVA

"Create in me a clean heart, O God; and renew a right spirit within me. Cast me not away from thy presence; and take not thy Holy Spirit from me. Restore unto me the joy of thy salvation; and uphold me with thy free Spirit."

Only a loyal Spirit can be thankful. A corrupt spirit does not appreciate a thing. With a thankful heart, your praise will be like an incense going directly to the Throne of God.

- Myrrh – Word

To have the undiluted word of God.

Joshua 1:8 KJV

"This book of the law shall not depart out of thy mouth; but thou shalt meditate therein day and night, that thou may observe to do according to all that is written therein: for then thou shalt make thy way prosperous, and then thou shalt have good success."

- Word is power. In your darkest time, the Word will console you.

Psalms 51:15 KJV

"O Lord, open thou my lips; and my mouth shall shew forth thy praise."

- Sanctified by the blood of Jesus Christ and made Holy for the work.

John 17:19 KJVA

"And for their sake I sanctify myself, that they also might be sanctified through the truth."

- Empowered by the Spirit of God. The Holy Spirit will give you the tools for the journey.

Act 1:8 KJVA

"But ye shall receive power, after that the Holy Ghost is come upon you: and ye shall be witnesses unto me both in Jerusalem, and in all Judea, and in Samaria, and unto the uttermost part of the earth."

You must possess these three things if you want to overcome the deceit of the devil. The ROD called the LIGHT OF GOD, which is the HOLY SPIRIT to lead you in your ways. INCENSE called PRAISE; It is the KEY that opens the spiritual realm to God. MYRRH, called The WORD, that consoles in times of sorrow; it enlightens and reveals God's purpose to man. These three things make you become an OVERCOMER.

CHAPTER TWO
FALSE PROMISE, PROPHECY AND VISION

I discussed it in the last chapter how Satan, the king of darkness, can disguise as light and his host as messengers of God to deceive man through man's selfish heart's desire.

James 4:1 KJVA
"From whence come wars and fightings among you? come they not hence, even of your lusts that war in your members?"

In this lesson, we will look at how Satan can penetrate with his deceit through man's inability to keep vowing and how man is always looking for ways to manipulate God into getting his desire, forgetting that you can not blackmail

God.

The First Book Of Adam and Eve Chap XXXII (32):1-8

1 AND Adam and Eve remained in the Cave of Treasures until the seventh day; they neither ate of the fruit of the earth, nor drank water.

2 And when it dawned on the eighth day, Adam said to Eve, "O Eve, we prayed God to give us somewhat from the garden, and He sent His angels who brought us what we had desired.

3 "But now, arise, let us go to the sea of water we saw at first, and let us stand in it, praying that God will again be favorable to us and take us back to the garden; or give us something; or that He will give us comfort in some other land than this in which we are."

4 Then Adam and Eve came out of the cave, went and stood on the border of the sea in which they had before thrown themselves, and Adam said to Eve.

5 "Come, go down into this place, and come not out of it until the end of thirty days, when I shall come to thee. And pray to God with fervent heart and a sweet voice, to forgive us.

6 "And I will go to another place, and go down into it, and do like thee."

7 Then Eve went down into the water, as Adam had commanded her. Adam also went down into the water; and they stood praying; and besought the Lord to forgive them their offence, and to restore them to their former state.

8 And they stood thus praying, unto the end of the five-and-thirty days.

We must look at these facts in human lives and ways before the coming of Satan into the picture.

- Man is never content with his position, always looking for ways to elevate himself, even though he may be in that position by God's wish.
- We do not observe some fasting and prayers in truth, some are being carried out through indirect deceit to force God in doing what man wants.
- Most times we lingered much on prayer already answered. That is why we stay in a position for so long, asking without getting results.

James 4:3 KJVA

"Ye ask, and receive not, because ye ask amiss, that ye may consume it upon your lusts."

False Promise, Prophecy or Vision

First Book Of Adam and Eve Chap. XXXIII: 1-8

1 BUT Satan, the hater of all good, sought them in the cave, but found them not, although he searched diligently for them.

2 But he found them standing in the water praying and thought within himself, "Adam and Eve are thus standing in that water beseeching God to forgive them their transgression, and to restore them to their former estate, and to take them from under my hand.

3 "But I will deceive them so that they shall come out of the water, and not fulfil their vow."

4 Then the hater of all good, went not to Adam, but be went to Eve, and took the form of an angel of God, praising and rejoicing, and said to her-

5 "Peace be unto thee! Be glad and rejoice! God is favorable unto you, and He sent me to Adam. I have brought him the glad tidings of salvation, and of his being filled with bright light as he was at first.

6 "And Adam, in his joy for his restoration, has sent me to thee, that thou come to me, in order that I crown thee with light like him.

7 "And he said to me, 'Speak unto Eve; if she does not come with thee, tell her of the sign when we were on the top of the mountain; how God sent His angels who took us

and brought us to the Cave of Treasures; and laid the gold on the southern side; incense, on the eastern side; and myrrh on the western side.' Now come to him."

8 When Eve heard these words from him, she rejoiced greatly. And thinking that Satan's appearance was real, she came out of the sea.

- Man's inability to keep vowing.

Satan knows that when man is in desperation, he eagerly makes a vow to get mercy, but when he has received his request, man will most likely forget the vow or fulfill it partially. During this vow, the devil will bring a false promise, prophecy or vision to the request in other to render the vow unfulfilled or abandon.

- Satan do seek and penetrate the naïve and gullible in faith and wisdom.

Satan knows that the weak in faith would not wait for confirmation from God, neither will he analyze the discrepancy of the Spirit or words with that of God's previous promise and ways.

Things to know from words of Satan:

- Satan's words are always attractive; too good to be true.
- Full of contradictions and lies.
- Impossible feast or quest to achieve.
- Satan is always talking about past deeds to lay his claims on and no specific words about the future.
- It never brings in Biblical solution except ones that go against the ways of God.
- His words always lead man astray from God, making man to abandon God's calling, vow and way.

In the discourse of Satan and Eve, Satan claimed to be sent by God to Adam, and in turn, Adam sent him to Eve.

- Angels of Light are messengers of God only. They are sent to man by God, to either deliver message to man or assist man by God's command.

These Angels do not run errands for man by man's request because they answer only to God. Man can only have access to them through the Father, Son and Holy Spirit.

- Demons (falling angels or angels of

darkness) are the ones that man can invoke. They run errands for man, claiming they are messengers for both God and man. These demons can be requested, invoked, or ordered to carry out man's requests or wishes. They can be manipulated because they have already lost their glory in God's kingdom and they are now with misplaced priorities.

Let's look at the case of Mary the mother of Jesus. Luke 1:26-27 KJVA

"And in the sixth month the angel Gabriel was sent from God unto a city of Galilee, named Nazareth, to a virgin espoused to a man whose name was Joseph, of the house of David; and the virgin's name was Mary."

God sent the angel Gabriel to Mary to deliver His message to her. She did not, in turn, send him to Joseph, knowing fully well that she was betrothed to him. God knows our past, present and future, so He already made provision for every area of our lives. God Himself sent His angel to Joseph to shed light on the state of Mary to him because Joseph had an authority over Mary based on God's rule and command, which placed husband as the head of the wife.

Matthew 1:20 KJVA

"But while he thought on these things, behold, the angel of the Lord appeared unto him in a dream, saying, Joseph, thou son of David, fear not to take unto thee Mary thy wife: for that which is conceived in her is of the Holy Ghost."

Overcoming False Promise, Prophecy or Vision.

- God will never contradict Himself. It is the word of Satan that always goes against rules laid down by God. With careful observation, easily will you see the deceit in the word of Satan.

James 1:19 KJVA

"Wherefore, my beloved brethren, let every man be swift to hear, slow to speak, slow to wrath:"

Do not be quick to accept neither judge because the devil is looking for whom to devour.

- The words of Satan will never acknowledge Jesus Christ as Lord. The spirit of darkness will only be interested in glorifying himself.

1 John 4:2-3 KJVA

"Hereby know ye the Spirit of God: Every spirit that

confess that Jesus Christ is come in the flesh is of God: and every spirit that confess not that Jesus Christ is come in the flesh is not of God: and this is that spirit of antichrist, whereof ye have heard that it should come; and even now already is it in the world."

Discern everything with calm observation and obedience to the Holy Spirit, and you will become an OVERCOMER.

CHAPTER THREE
TRIALS, TEMPTATIONS AND TRIBULATIONS

Look at Christendom today, many children of God are ignorantly under the torment of the devil which is not supposed to be. Many turned to regard the trials, temptation and tribulations coming their ways as tests from God, which is not true.

Truly, God takes us through a journey of faith, which is called the Lesson of Life. This examines our strength, belief and trust and to determine the level of our faith and loyalty we have in Him, but this journey is never hurtful.

God tested Abraham in ...

Genesis 22:1-9 AMP
"Now after these things, God tested [the faith and

commitment of] Abraham and said to him, "Abraham!" And he answered, "Here I am." God said, "Take now your son, your only son [of promise], whom you love, Isaac, and go to the region of Moriah, and offer him there as a burnt offering on one of the mountains of which I shall tell you.

So Abraham got up early in the morning, saddled his donkey, and took two of his young men with him and his son Isaac; and he split the wood for the burnt offering, and then he got up and went to the place of which God had told him. On the third day [of travel] Abraham looked up and saw the place in the distance. Abraham said to his servants, "Settle down and stay here with the donkey; the young man and I will go over there and worship [God], and we will come back to you." Then Abraham took the wood for the burnt offering and laid it on [the shoulders of] Isaac his son, and he took the fire (firepot) in his own hand and the [sacrificial] knife; and the two of them walked on together. And Isaac said to Abraham, "My father!" And he said, "Here I am, my son." Isaac said, "Look, the fire and the wood, but where is the lamb for the burnt offering?" Abraham said, "My son, God will provide for Himself a lamb for the burnt offering." So the two walked on together. When they came to the place of which God had told him, Abraham built an altar there and arranged the wood, and bound Isaac his son and placed him on the altar, on top of the wood."

God asked Abraham to sacrifice his only beloved son while his wife, Sarah, was already advanced in age. God did this to test his level of love and loyalty Abraham had for Him, but at the end, this test was never to harm Isaac or hurt Abraham.

Just like Jesus was in the boat with his disciples.

Matthew 8:23-25 KJV.

"And when he was entered into a ship, his disciples followed him. And, behold, there arose a great tempest in the sea, insomuch that the ship was covered with the waves: but he was asleep. And his disciples came to him, and awoke him, saying, Lord, save us: we perish."

Jesus was sleeping in the boat because of His human body and nature which needed rest in order to function well and while he was sleeping in the physical even though His spirit never sleeps, storm came heavily on them and the disciples were afraid despite all the miracles Jesus Christ had performed in front of them. This storm was just a test of their faith, God the Son wanted to know if these people really knew how mighty He was because you can not have God the Son with you who is the creator of all things and storm of life should overwhelm you.

John 1:1-4 AMP

"In the beginning [before all time] was the Word (Christ), and the Word was with God, and the Word was God Himself. He was [continually existing] in the beginning [co-eternally] with God. All things were made and came into existence through Him; and without Him not even one thing was made that has come into being. In Him was life [and the power to bestow life], and the life was the Light of men."

This made it impossible for the sea, wave, storm, or any other elements to go against Him, neither is it possible for the storm to overturn His boat. But His disciples could not understand this simple logic.

Matthew 8:26 KJV

"And he saith unto them, Why are ye fearful, O ye of little faith? Then he arose, and rebuked the winds and the sea; and there was a great calm."

For anyone going into a test of faith, know that it is for a purpose, the disciples refused to acknowledge their right in Christ by commanding the storm to be still through the name of Jesus, but if they could have done that, they would have received authority to walk over principalities and power of darkness right there and then. A test of faith is to bring out our potential in Christ so that we will do more exploits.

Let us look at the torment that Satan brought upon Adam and Eve and then compare it with God's chastised.

TRIALS, TEMPTATIONS AND TRIBULATIONS OF SATAN THAT LOOK LIKE GOD'S CHASTISE.

First Book Of Adam and Eve Chap. XLIII (43):1-16

1 THEN Adam and Eve were afraid, and stood still. And Adam said to Eve, "What is that fire by our cave? We do nothing in it to bring about this fire.

2 "We neither have bread to bake therein, nor broth to cook there. As to this fire, we know not the like, neither do we know what to call it.

3 "But ever since God sent the cherub with a sword of fire that flashed and lightened in his hand, from fear of which we fell down and were like corpses, have we not seen the like.

4 "But now O Eve, behold, this is the same fire that

was in the cherub's hand, which God has sent to keep the cave in which we dwell.

5 "O Eve, it is because God is angry with us, and will drive us from it.

6 "O Eve, we have again transgressed His commandment in that cave, so that He had sent this fire to burn around it, and to prevent us from going into it.

7 "If this be really so, O Eve, where shall we dwell? And whither shall we flee from before the face of the Lord? Since, as regards the garden, He will not let us abide in it, and He has deprived us of the good things thereof; but He has placed us in this cave, in which we have borne darkness, trials and hardships, until at last we found comfort therein.

8 "But now that He has brought us out into another land, who knows what may happen in it? And who knows but that the darkness of that land may be far greater than the darkness of this land?

9 "Who knows what may happen in that land by day or by night? And who knows whether it will be far or near, O Eve? Where it will please God to put us, may be far from the garden, O Eve! or where God will prevent us from beholding Him, because we have transgressed His commandment, and because we have made requests unto Him at all times?

10 "O Eve, if God will bring us into a strange land other than this, in which we find consolation, it must be to put our souls to death, and blot out our name from the face of the earth.

11 "O Eve, if we are farther estranged from the garden and from God, where shall we find Him again, and ask Him to give us gold, incense, myrrh, and some fruit of the fig-tree?

12 "Where shall we find Him, to comfort us a second time? Where shall we find Him, that He may think of us, as regards the covenant He has made on our behalf T'

13 Then Adam said no more. And they kept looking, he and Eve, towards the cave, and at the fire that flared up around it.

14 But that fire was from Satan. For he had gathered trees and dry grasses, and had carried and brought them to the cave, and had set fire to them, in order to consume the cave and--what was in it.

15 So that Adam and Eve should be left in sorrow, and he should cut off their trust in God, and make them deny Him.

16 But by the mercy of God he could not burn the cave, for God sent His angel round the cave to guard it from such a fire, until it went out.

Trials, temptation and tribulation come because of our disobedience, which the devil uses to inflict man, and he brought these 3Ts to man by...

- Lamentation

The more we lament of our predicament, the more our situation worsens because the devil capitalized on our weakness to inflict more sorrow.

- Self reliance

This always brings man to a destructive end, just like Samson. It was God's plan for Samson to liberate his people from the hand of the Philistine...

Judges 13:5 KJV

"For, lo, thou shalt conceive, and bear a son; and no razor shall come on his head: for the child shall be a Nazarite unto God from the womb: and he shall begin to deliver Israel out of the hand of the Philistines."

...but it was Samson doing that he went into the captivity of the enemies. He consciously walked into the trap of the devil by deceit of love and lust, which was brought by Delilah.

Judges 16:4-7 KJV

"And it came to pass afterward, that he loved a woman in the valley of Sorek, whose name was Delilah. And the lords of the Philistines came up unto her, and said unto her, Entice him, and see wherein his great strength lieth, and by what means we may prevail against him, that we may bind him to afflict him: and we will give thee every one of us eleven hundred pieces of silver. And Delilah said to Samson, Tell me, I pray thee, wherein thy great strength lieth, and wherewith thou mightest be bound to afflict thee. And Samson said unto her, If they bind me with seven green that were never dried, then shall I be weak, and be as another man"

Samson's unwillingness to walk away from temptation of lust and his self reliance, which is overconfidence in oneself and not on God, who is the Ultimate Protector, landed him in a great tribulation.

Judges 16:20-21 KJV

"And she said, The Philistines be upon thee, Samson. And he awoke out of his sleep, and said, I will go out as at other times before, and shake myself.

And he wist not that the Lord was departed from him. But the Philistines took him, and put out his eyes, and brought him down to Gaza, and bound him with fetters of brass; and he did grind in the prison house."

He got to a stage that he was self reliant on himself. He left his people and went after foreign women in a foreign land. It was there that he got tempted by Delilah into divulging his secret and this resulted in his tribulations in the land of the Philistines.

James 1:13-14 KJVA

"Let no man say when he is tempted, I am tempted of God: for God cannot be tempted with evil, neither tempt he any man: (14) but every man is tempted, when he is drawn away of his own lust, and enticed."

God does not chastise his children with death or sickness, but the devil will make it look like a punishment from God and ironically, man accepts this fate, thereby putting the blame on God. It was Satan that brought tribulations on Job and not God. Yes, God gave Satan permission to test Job and Job also never complained because he believed the test was from God.

Job 1:21 KJV

"And said, Naked came I out of my mother's womb, and naked shall I return thither: the Lord gave, and the Lord hath taken away; blessed be the name of the Lord."

Job accepted the calamity Satan was handling out to him, but when he was on the point of breaking, he cursed the day he was born. If he had known that the catastrophe was from Satan, Job would have rebuked Satan right from the start. God's chastise is a rebuke for our wrong ways, and it is to draw us back to God.

Let us look at Jonah...

Jonah 1:1-4 KJV

"Now the word of the Lord came unto Jonah the son of Amittai, saying, Arise, go to Nineveh, that great city, and cry against it; for their wickedness is come up before me.

But Jonah rose up to flee unto Tarshish from the presence of the Lord, and went down to Joppa; and he found a ship going to Tarshish: so he paid the fare thereof, and went down into it, to go with them unto Tarshish from the presence of the Lord. But the Lord sent out a great wind into the sea, and there was a mighty tempest in the sea, so that the ship was like to be broken."

Jonah was disobedient to the message of God By trying to run away from God's appointment, hence his stay in the fish's belly for three days.

Jonah 2:1-4 KJV
"Then Jonah prayed unto the Lord his God out of the fish's belly, And said, I cried by reason of mine affliction unto the Lord, and he heard me; out of the belly of hell cried I, and thou heardest my voice. For thou hadst cast me into the deep, in the midst of the seas; and the floods compassed me about: all thy billows and thy waves passed over me. Then I said, I am cast out of thy sight; yet I will look again toward thy holy temple."

In the end, his stay was to bring him back to his senses and plan of God. A good father discipline his child whenever the child goes astray, but the chastise is never to death but to bring back the child to the right path.

Overcoming The Trials, Temptation and Tribulation of Satan.

- Understanding situations.

When you calmly understand what you are passing through, if there is a lesson to learn from it or it is a battle of life which is hurting you, then you will hasten to free yourself from the devil. Immediately you understand it is a battle, that your predicament hurts, then you rebuke the devil fast before he brings more woes.

Matthew 18:18 KJV

"Verily I say unto you, Whatsoever ye shall bind on earth shall be bound in heaven: and whatsoever ye shall loose on earth shall be loosed in heaven."

- Know your stand in Christ

1 John 4:4 KJVA

"Ye are of God, little children, and have overcome them: because greater is he that is in you, than he that is in the world."

When you have the life in you, that is when you can freely command the devil and he will flee.

Philippians 2:9-11 KJV

"Wherefore God also hath highly exalted him, and

given him a name which is above every name: That at the name of Jesus every knee should bow, of things in heaven, and things in earth, and things under the earth; And that every tongue should confess that Jesus Christ is Lord, to the glory of God the Father."

But for anyone to use the name of Jesus Christ successfully, you have to be fully in Christ so you do not fall into affliction of Satan more like the children of Sceva in ...

Acts 19:11-16 KJV

"And God wrought special miracles by the hands of Paul: So that from his body were brought unto the sick handkerchiefs or aprons, and the diseases departed from them, and the evil spirits went out of them.

Then certain of the vagabond Jews, exorcists, took upon them to call over them which had evil spirits the name of the Lord Jesus, saying,

We adjure you by Jesus whom Paul preached. And there were seven sons of one Sceva, a Jew, and chief of the priests, which did so. And the evil spirit answered and said, Jesus I know, and Paul I know; but who are ye? And the man in whom the evil spirit was leaped on them, and overcame them, and prevailed against them, so that they fled out of that house naked and wounded."

A true being in Christ has an authority to stop the torment of Satan.
- There will always be tribulations, but be courageous.

Jesus made us to understand this simple fact because the devil is in this world and he is there to kill, steal and destroy, but if you are in Christ, then the devil can not overpower you.

John 16:33 KJVA
"These things I have spoken unto you, that in me ye might have peace. In the world ye shall have tribulation: but be of good cheer; I have overcome the world.

- There must be faith to overcome.

Hebrews 11:6 KJVA
"But without faith it is impossible to please him: for he that cometh to God must believe that he is, and that he

is a rewarder of them that diligently seek him."

A faithless man's prayer can not be answered because he already doubted the ability of God to do that which he asked for. The book of James describes such a person as.

James 1:6-8 KJVA
"But let him ask in faith, nothing wavering: for he that waver is like a wave of the sea driven with the wind and tossed. For let not that man think that he shall receive any thing of the Lord. A double-minded man is unstable in all his ways."

A double-minded man who does not know what he really wants. God has no use for a confused person because such a person is halfway in God and halfway in the world already.

Beloved, for Christ to fight your battle for you, you have to be fully committed to Him.

Matthew 26:41 KJVA
"Watch and pray, that ye enter not into temptation: the spirit indeed is willing, but the flesh is weak."

The disciples experienced storm, but with Him in the boat, the storm could not overthrow them. All they needed was to call on Jesus to save them. To be an OVERCOMER over storms of life, all you need is to call on Him with confidence. He is always ready to save you.

CHAPTER FOUR

ALTERNATE ROUTE OFFER – A SHORTCUT

Every man has a purpose in life, for an existence there must be a mission and a target to reach and at the end of any race, there must surely be a reward to collect.

2 Timothy 4:7-8 KJVA

"I have fought a good fight, I have finished my course, I have kept the faith: (8) henceforth there is laid up for me a crown of righteousness, which the Lord, the righteous judge, shall give me at that day: and not to me only, but unto all them also that love his appearing."

Just like man, the devil is also running a race to populate his kingdom to bring destruction to man.

1 Peter 5:8 KJVA

"Be sober, be vigilant; because your adversary the devil, as a roaring lion, walketh about, seeking whom he may devour:"

Satan does not want man to achieve his goals neither does he want man to be saved because the devil himself is cursed and damnation in the Hades is his fate, hence he is looking for whom to be part of his suffering in hell.

First Book Of Adam & Eve Chap. LX (60) :1-2

1 THEN on the eighty-ninth day, Satan came to the cave, clad in a garment of light, and girt about with a bright girdle.

2 In his hands was a staff of light, and he looked most awful: but his face was pleasant and his speech was sweet.

- Not all that glitters are gold.

God already has a plan for man, but there must be a path to follow, lessons to learn and work to be done before getting the reward.

Ecclesiastes 3:2-9 KJVA

2 "A time to be born, and a time to die; a time to plant,

and a time to pluck up that which is planted; (3) a time to kill, and a time to heal; a time to break down, and a time to build up;

(4) a time to weep, and a time to laugh; a time to mourn, and a time to dance;

(5) a time to cast away stones, and a time to gather stones together; a time to embrace, and a time to refrain from embracing;

(6) a time to get, and a time to lose; a time to keep, and a time to cast away;

(7) a time to rend, and a time to sew; a time to keep silence, and a time to speak;

(8) a time to love, and a time to hate; a time of war, and a time of peace.

(9) What profit hath he that worketh in that wherein he laboreth?"

This passage makes us to understand that there is a time for very thing under the earth. Before you can be rewarded, there must be a labor, but it is during this labor that the devil will bring in a false reward, a make-believe glory from an alternative route which is always quicker and faster than the path of God. God's path is like a farm where you have to cut and clear the grass, dig the ribs, plant the crops, water what you have planted, then wait for the crops to grow, then harvest. God's route takes patience, but in the end, there is a reward.

First Book Of Adam and Eve Chap. LX (60):3-6

3 He thus transformed himself in order to deceive Adam and Eve, and to make them come out of the cave, ere they had fulfilled the forty days.

4 For he said within himself, "Now that when they had fulfilled the forty days' fasting and praying, God would restore them to their former estate; but if He did not do so, He would still be favourable to them; and even if He had not mercy on them, would He yet give them something from the garden to comfort them; as already twice before."

5 Then Satan drew near the cave in this fair appearance, and said.

6 "O Adam, rise ye, stand up, thou and Eve, and come along with me, to a good land; and fear not. I am flesh and bones like you; and at first I was a creature that God created.

- Offer of Satan is always enticing and sounds better.

Some will seem faster to achieve, but at the end of

the day, there will be regrets. Satan's offer will come out of a make-believe consign to one's plight, but it is just a pretense to lead one astray.

- Satan will seem heartbroken, painting God as a betrayal.

First Book Of Adam and Eve Chap. LX (60):7-13

7 "And it was so, that when He had created me, He placed me in a garden in the north, on the border of the world.

8 "And He said to me, 'Abide here!' And I abode there according to His Word, neither did I transgress His commandment.

9 "Then He made a slumber to come over me, and He brought thee, O Adam, out of my side, but did not make thee abide by me.

10 "But God took thee in His divine hand, and placed thee in a garden to the eastward.

11 "Then I grieved because of thee, for that while God had taken thee out of my side, He had not let thee abide with me.

12 "But God said unto me: 'Grieve not because of Adam, whom I brought out of thy side; no harm will come

to him.

13 "'For now I have brought out of his side a helpmeet for him; and I have given him joy by so doing.'"

In the passage above, he seemed heartbroken by God's betrayal and abandonment. Indirectly telling Adam that God was not consigned about Adam's plight because he was not the first person to be used and dumped.

Proverbs 26:22-24 KJVA

22 "The words of a talebearer are as wounds, and they go down into the innermost parts of the belly.

23 Burning lips and a wicked heart are like a potsherd covered with silver dross.

24 He that hateth dissembleth with his lips, and layeth up deceit within him;"

He painted himself as someone who was loyal and humble to God, who believed everything God says but was later forgotten by God when Adam came to the picture.

- Satan brings in favoritism into the picture.

Ephesians 6:8-9 KJV

"knowing that whatsoever good thing any man doeth,

the same shall he receive of the Lord, whether he be bond or free. And, ye masters, do the same things unto them, forbearing threatening: knowing that your Master also is in heaven; neither is there respect of persons with him."

God is not partial to anyone, He hates favoritism. God is only consign with our heart, once He sees a pure heart, you become God's own but if your heart is defiled and full of evil, you then become an enemy of God because you have already aligned yourself with God's enemy which is Satan. It is this that the devil capitalized on to paint God as unjust.

Romans 9:13-14 KJVA

"As it is written, Jacob have I loved, but Esau have I hated. What shall we say then? Is there unrighteousness with God? God forbid."

These words do not just come out. Jacob always does the ish of God, which his parents attested to, and Esau is nonchalant in attitude. Esau ways displeased his father.

Genesis 28:6-9 KJVA

"When Esau saw that Isaac had blessed Jacob, and

sent him away to Pa´dan–a´ram, to take him a wife from thence; and that as he blessed him he gave him a charge, saying, Thou shalt not take a wife of the daughters of Canaan;

7 and that Jacob obeyed his father and his mother, and was gone to Pa´dan–a´ram;

8 and Esau seeing that the daughters of Canaan pleased not Isaac his father;

9 then went Esau unto Ish´ma-el, and took unto the wives which he had Ma´halath the daughter of Ish´ma-el Abraham's son, the sister of Neba´joth, to be his wife."

God can never love a disobedient child because disobedience goes against the ways of God. Before the time of Isaac, it had already been a warning to the children of Abraham not to mix with the Canaanite because of their foreign gods-idolatry. But Esau still finds them attractive and even after hearing his father's words to Jacob, he did not go to the father for forgiveness and ask for direction of what he wants. This shows a rebelliousness and non-regard for his parents. This behavior brings out the saying "Jacob I love (his ways please me), Esau I hate" (his ways do not please me. I hate his ways).

1 Samuel 15:22-23 KJVA

"And Samuel said, Hath the Lord as great delight in burnt offerings and sacrifices, as in obeying the voice of the Lord? Behold, to obey is better than sacrifice, and to hearken than the fat of rams.

23 For rebellion is as the sin of witchcraft, and stubbornness is as iniquity and idolatry. Because thou hast rejected the word of the Lord, he hath also rejected thee from being king."

Because of our disobedience, not wanting to do the right thing and wait for the right time, Satan turns to turn man from the right route to the alternative route leading to destruction

First Book Of Adam and Eve Chap. LX (60) :14-17

14 Then Satan said again, "I did not know how it is ye are in this cave, nor anything about this trial that has come upon you-until God said to me, 'Behold, Adam has transgressed, he whom I had taken out of thy side, and Eve also, whom I took out of his side; and I have driven them out of the garden; I have made them dwell in a land of sorrow and misery, because they transgressed against Me, and have hearkened to Satan. And lo, they are in suffering

unto this day, the eightieth.'

15 "Then God said unto me, 'Arise, go to them, and make them come to thy place, and suffer not that Satan come near them, and afflict them. For they are now in great misery; and lie helpless from hunger.'

16 "He further said to me, 'When thou hast taken them to thyself, give them to eat of the fruit of the Tree of Life, and give them to drink of the water of peace; and clothe them in a garment of light, and restore them to their former state of grace, and leave them not in misery, for they came from thee. But grieve not over them, nor repent of that which has come upon them.'

17 "But when I heard this, I was sorry; and my heart could not patiently bear it for thy sake, O my child.

- The first thing we should know is that God is Self Sufficient (El Shaddai).

Philippians 4:19 KJVA

"But my God shall supply all your need according to his riches in glory by Christ Jesus."

He does not need man's help to do whatever he desires. He is Al-Possible. It is man that needs God and not the other way round. In this passage, Satan-Old man claimed that God needs him to rescue Adam and Eve and to bring them to their former self even though he seemed helpless at first.

First Book of Adam and Eve Chap. LX (60) :26-29

26 "And now O my children, Adam and Eve, look at my hoar hairs and at my feeble estate, and at my coming from that distant place. Come, come with me, to a place of rest."

27 Then he began to weep and to sob before Adam and Eve, and his tears poured upon the earth like water.

28 And when Adam and Eve raised their eyes and saw his beard, and heard his sweet talk, their hearts softened towards him; they hearkened unto him, for they believed he was true.

29 And it seemed to them that they really were his offspring, when they saw that his face was like their own; and they trusted him.

- Makes use of emotional speech.

Satan can also play on our emotions to weaken our spirit. Do not allow the devil to unsettle your spirit else you will make a mistake.

Philippians 4:6 KJV

"Be careful for nothing; but in every thing by prayer and supplication with thanksgiving let your requests be made known unto God."

For a prayer to be answered, we must have the above points; Patience, Faith and Courage. When we have these three things, then we should pray to God and thank Him for prayer already answered. We must not pray as someone doubting the capability of the prayer, hence we render it useless, but with confidence in the power of God, we can achieve the aim of God for our lives.

Matthew 7:7-8 KJV

"Ask, and it shall be given you; seek, and ye shall find; knock, and it shall be opened unto you: (8) for every one that ask receive; and he that seek find; and to him that knock it shall be opened."

It is a promise of God which must be fulfilled as long as we ask in accordance with the will of God. Likewise, when we ask for his help, He will definitely come to our rescue. When God on your side, what can man or the devil do to you? Always call on God in any situation you are in, be it good or bad, and He will help you in time of trouble. With the help of God, we are OVERCOMERS

CHAPTER FIVE
ANOTHER BETTER PLAN

First Book Of Adam and Eve Chap. LXVII (67):1-7

1 But when Adam and Eve went down to the land of black mud, and came near to the wheat God had showed them, and saw it ripe and ready for reaping, as they had no sickle to reap it withal--they girt themselves, and began to pull up the wheat, until it was all done.

2 Then they made it into a heap; and, faint from heat and from thirst, they went under a shady tree, where the breeze fanned them to sleep.

3 But Satan saw what Adam and Eve had done. And he called his hosts, and said to them, "Since God has shown to Adam and Eve all about this wheat, wherewith to strengthen their bodies--and, lo, they are come and have made a heap of it, and faint from the toil are now asleep--

come, let us set fire to this heap of corn, and burn it, and let us take that bottle of water that is by them, and empty it out, so that they may find nothing to drink, and we kill them with hunger and thirst.

4 "Then, when they wake up from their sleep, and seek to return to the cave, we will come to them in the way, and will lead them astray; so that they die of hunger and thirst; when they may, perhaps, deny God, and He destroy them. So shall we be rid of them."

5 Then Satan and his hosts threw fire upon the wheat and consumed it.

6 But from the heat of the flame Adam and Eve awoke from their sleep, and saw the wheat burning, and the bucket of water by them, poured out.

7 Then they wept and went back to the cave.

- God does not make mistakes.

We must understand that before God can give us a plan, He must have perfected it. He never makes an error.

Jeremiah 29:11 KJVA

"For I know the thoughts that I think toward you, saith the Lord, thoughts of peace, and not of evil, to give you an expected end."

God is love, and He loves His children. When He created man, He created man in His own image by breathing into his (man) nostrils.

Genesis 2:7-8 KJVA

"And the Lord God formed man of the dust of the ground, and breathed into his nostrils the breath of life; and man became a living soul. And the Lord God planted a garden eastward in Eden; and there he put the man whom he had formed."

By this breath, we become like God in our thinking and attributes. He gave us ability to reason like Him, then He placed man in the Garden Of Delight (Eden) for man to enjoy the good things of God's work but because of the deceit of the devil in a serpent's body, Satan could deceive Eve, bringing fall to man. Man became unclean by disobedience to God's commandment, thereby unfit to stay in the garden. Despite that, they consigned God. He does not want us to perish, that is why the Bible says...

John 3:16-17 KJVA

"For God so loved the world, that he gave his only

begotten Son, that whosoever believe in him should not perish, but have everlasting life.

17 For God sent not his Son into the world to condemn the world; but that the world through him might be saved."

The purpose of Jesus Christ coming to earth is to save us from our sin. Satan became aware of this and he does not want man to return to the lost glory.

Just like Satan destroyed the Wheat Of Adam and Eve, he is also destroying callings, homes, works, countries and people because of his jealousy for anything good. He so much hate good things.

The First Book Of Adam and Eve Chap. LXVII (67):7-12

7 Then they wept and went back to the cave.

8 But as they were going up from below the mountain where they were, Satan and his hosts met them in the form of angels, praising God.

9 Then Satan said to Adam, "O Adam, why art thou so pained with hunger and thirst? It seems to me that Satan has burnt up the wheat." And Adam said to him, "Ay."

10 Again Satan said to Adam, "Come back with us; we

are angels of God. God sent us to thee, to show thee another field of corn, better than that; and beyond it is a fountain of good water, and many trees, where thou shalt dwell near it, and work the corn-field to better purpose than that which Satan has consumed."

11 Adam thought that he was true, and that they were angels who talked with him; and he went back with them.

12. Then Satan began to lead astray Adam and Eve eight days, until they both fell down as if dead, from hunger, thirst, and faintness. Then he fled with his hosts, and left them.

- Sorrow comes from Satan.

Just like he destroyed their wheat and caused them sorrow, he is also causing havoc for man. It does not matter who you are; be it Pastor, Mechanic, Student or Philosopher. No matter the field you are in or your status in society, as long as you are happy, Satan will work to bring sorrow to you because he despises happiness.

- Offer a false solution and better plan.

When he destroys, he will also be the one to console. After he burnt their wheat, he came to offer them a better field, claiming he is an angel of God.

We already analyzed how the hosts of darkness will disguise as angels of God to lead astray. Angel of God will never offer a plan different from that of God. Any prophecy, dream or vision that is contrary to God's word is from the devil. Also, any advice or idea that goes against the rule of God is satanic.

Proverbs 12:6-7 KJVA
"The words of the wicked are to lie in wait for blood: but the mouth of the upright shall deliver them. The wicked are overthrown, and are not: but the house of the righteous shall stand."

A friend can give advice to you with a consigned face, but most of the advice goes against the word of God, the law of the state or country, know that it is satanic. Only an evil advice can be rebellious, it does not matter if it sounds relieving.

Psalm 1:1 KJV
"Blessed is the man that walk not in the counsel of the ungodly, nor stand in the way of sinners, nor sit in the

seat of the scornful."

Overcoming a deceitful plan.
- Familiarity with the word of God.

Joshua 1:8 KJV

"This book of the law shall not depart out of thy mouth; but thou shalt meditate therein day and night, that thou mayest observe to do according to all that is written therein: for then thou shalt make thy way prosperous, and then thou shalt have good success."

Studying the word of God brings familiarity, understanding and foreknowledge of the evil plan of Satan. It is by studying that the Holy Spirit reveals things of God to man. He will make known plans of Satan and also guide our steps so we do not go astray.

- Intimacy with God.

By continuous fellowship with God, we come closer to Him and to know His wishes, making it difficult for Satan to lead us astray. By being intimate with God, we know His dos and don'ts. We become doers of His words and not hearers only.

James 1:22-25 KJV

"But be ye doers of the word, and not hearers only, deceiving your own selves.

(23) For if any be a hearer of the word, and not a doer, he is like unto a man beholding his natural face in a glass:

(24) for he behold himself, and goe his way, and straightway forget what manner of man he was. But whoso look into the perfect law of liberty, and continue therein, he being not a forgetful hearer,

(25) but a doer of the work, this man shall be blessed in his deed."

Becoming like Christ and living in righteousness, doing things pleasing to God, we become untouchable to Satan since we are God's children. He builds an edge around us, making no evil befall us, though we may see it, but it will not overpower us.

Psalm 91:1-7, 9-14 KJVA

"He that dwell in the secret place of the Most High shall abide under the shadow of the Almighty.

2 I will say of the Lord, He is my refuge and my fortress: my God; in him will I trust.

3 Surely he shall deliver thee from the snare of the fowler, and from the noisome pestilence.

4 He shall cover thee with his feathers, and under his wings shalt thou trust: his truth shall be thy shield and buckler.

5 Thou shalt not be afraid for the terror by night; nor for the arrow that fly by day;

6 nor for the pestilence that walk in darkness; nor for the destruction that waste at noonday.

7 A thousand shall fall at thy side, and ten thousand at thy right hand; but it shall not come nigh thee.

8 "Only with thine eyes shalt thou behold and see the reward of the wicked."

9 Because thou hast made the Lord, which is my refuge, even the Most High, thy habitation;

10 there shall no evil befall thee, neither shall any plague come nigh thy dwelling.

11 For he shall give his angels charge over thee, to keep thee in all thy ways.

12 They shall bear thee up in their hands, lest thou dash thy foot against a stone.

13 Thou shalt tread upon the lion and adder: the young lion and the dragon shalt thou trample under feet.

14 Because he hath set his love upon me, therefore

will I deliver him.

Living godly lives only can deliver us from diverting from the good and straight path. You will remain OVERCOMER.

CHAPTER SIX
AGREEMENT BY COMPULSION

God gave man the ability to reason by breathing into his nostrils, giving man liberty in what he does. God created edible fruits in the garden along with forbidden fruit.

Genesis 2:9 KJV
"And out of the ground made the Lord God to grow every tree that is pleasant to the sight, and good for food; the tree of life also in the midst of the garden, and the tree of knowledge of good and evil."

The purpose of these trees is for man to choose to follow God's commandment willingly. God does not force His will on us, neither does He want us to follow Him grudgingly.

John 6:51 KJVA

"I am the living bread which came down from heaven: if any man eat of this bread, he shall live for ever: and the bread that I will give is my flesh, which I will give for the life of the world."

The 'if' signifies option: you either take it or leave it. If you eat it (accepting Jesus); you live (living spiritually in eternal life). If you don't eat (reject it); you unknowingly accept Satan and condemned with the devil. Jesus does not force Himself on man.

The First Book Of Adam and Eve Chap. LXX (70):1-16

AFTER this Satan, the hater of all good, took the form n angel, and with him two others, so that they looked like the three angels who had brought to Adam gold, incense, and myrrh.

2 They passed before Adam and Eve while they were under the tree, and greeted Adam and Eve with fair words that were full of guile.

3 But when Adam and Eve saw their comely mien, and heard their sweet speech, Adam rose, welcomed them, and brought them to Eve, and they remained all together;

Adam's heart the while, being glad because he thought concerning them, that they were the same angels, who had brought him gold, incense, and myrrh.

4 Because, when they came to Adam the first time, there came upon him from them, peace and joy, through their bringing him good tokens; so Adam thought that they were come a second time to give him other tokens for him to rejoice withal. For he did not know it was Satan; therefore did he receive them with joy and companied with them.

5 Then Satan, the tallest of them, said, "Rejoice, O Adam, and be glad. Lo, God has sent us to thee to tell thee something."

6 And Adam said, "What is it?" Then Satan answered, "It is a light thing, yet it is a word of God, wilt thou hear it from us and do it? But if thou hear not, we will return to God, and tell Him that thou would not receive His word."

And Satan said again to Adam, "Fear not, neither let a trembling come upon thee; dost not thou know us?"

8 But Adam said, "I know you not."

9 Then Satan said to him, "I am the angel who brought thee gold, and took it to the cave; this other one is he who brought thee incense; and that third one, is he who brought thee myrrh when thou wast on the top of the

mountain, and who carried thee to the cave.

10 "But as to the other angels our fellows, who bare you to the cave, God has not sent them with us this time; for He said to us, 'You suffice.'"

11 So when Adam heard these words he believed them, and said to these angels, "Speak the word of God, that I may receive it."

12 And Satan said unto him "Swear, and promise me that thou wilt receive it."

13 Then Adam said, "I know not how to swear and promise."

14 And Satan said to him, "Hold out thy hand, and put it inside my hand."

15 Then Adam held out his hand, and put it into Satan's hand; when Satan said unto him, "Say, now--so true as God is living, rational, and speaking, who raised the heavens in the space, and established the earth upon the waters, and has created me out of the four elements, and out of the dust of the earth--I will not break my promise, nor renounce my word."

16 And Adam swore thus.

- Satan enters through the known.

For Satan to penetrate a man, he must show himself in a known way, either through a friend, business, gift, offer, anything he knows that man will be comfortable with. By the comfort of his appearance channel, the man gets relaxed with him. He then penetrates when the spirit is weak.

In the passage, he appeared to Adam as a known angel. He knew what they were looking forward to: another visit from these angels to receive through them from God. Satan and his hosts disguised in order to penetrate Adam and Eve. Likewise, agents of Satan in today's time come as God's people with friendly smiles and they penetrate children of God. Their sweet tongues have corrupted many spirit-filled ministers of God. These agents of the devil offer misleading counsel. Their counsel sounds like a breakthrough to a frustrating situation. When not careful or strong in the Faith and in spirit, you may get derailed.

- Swearing is of the devil.

James 5:12 KJV

"But above all things, my brethren, swear not, neither by heaven, neither by the earth, neither by any other oath: but let your yea be yea; and your nay, nay; lest ye fall into condemnation."

Any agreement that requires you to swear by force is bad. God can not bring a word to his children and ask them to swear or accept it by force. Many Pastors of nowadays ask their members to make a compulsory vow or covenant before requesting a thing from God for their prayer to be answered in their church. This is not of God because it is not by your vow that God answered your prayer.

Romans 9:15-16 KJV
"For he saith to Moses, I will have mercy on whom I will have mercy, and I will have compassion on whom I will have compassion. So then it is not of him that will, nor of him that run, but of God that show mercy."

God favors whoever He wishes. Any vow a man makes must come from the heart and not by the compulsion of your pastor. Vow by compulsion does not serve the interests of God, but of your pastor. It is a deceitful vow.

Colossians 2:8 KJV
"Beware lest any man spoil you through philosophy and vain deceit, after the tradition of men, after the

rudiments of the world, and not after Christ."

Satan brings deceit with swearing as to bring man into bondage under him. By swearing, a man has entered a covenant with the devil. It is only God that can save such a man.

The First Book Of Adam and Eve Chap. LXXI(71):1-3

BUT when Adam heard these words from Satan, he sorrowed much, because of his oath and of his promise, and said, "Shall I commit adultery with my flesh and my bones, and shall I sin against myself, for God to destroy me, and to blot me out from off the face of the earth?

2 "Since, when at first, I ate of the tree, He drove me out of the garden into this strange land, and deprived me of my bright nature, and brought death upon me. If, then, I should do this, He will cut off my life from the earth, and He will cast me into hell, and will plague me there a long time.

3 "But God never spoke the words thou hast told me; and ye are not God's angels, nor yet sent from Him. But ye are devils, come to me under the false appearance of angels. Away from me; ye cursed of God!"

- Regret comes after a swear.

There is always a feeling of regret when you agree to do a thing by compulsion. A feeling of guilt and hurt will follow a swear after you realized you should have not. Compulsion leads one astray. It will only take you to where you do not bargain for, it captures your soul and continues to torment it. You only then reap the consequence and the other person will be let free. You alone bear the brute.

Overcoming agreement by compulsion.
- Be careful of who you let in.

2 Corinthians 11:13-14 KJV

"For such are false apostles, deceitful workers, transforming themselves into the apostles of Christ. (14) And no marvel; for Satan himself is transformed into an angel of light."

Do not believe everything you are told, always confirm it yourself with God. For God to send a message to you His child, He must have told you first through a form of communication you are familiar with, the message from a third party will be a confirmation of your revelation. But when a third party delivers a strange message to you, it is then that you should be consigned and careful to give into it. No matter the message, no one must not force it on you.

Jeremiah 23:16 KJV

"Thus saith the Lord of hosts, Hearken not unto the words of the (false) prophets that prophesy unto you; they make you vain: they speak a vision of their own heart, and not out of the mouth of the Lord."

- Investigate before agreement.

Search thoroughly before you agree to anything. Know what it entails so that you do not fall into the captivity of Satan. Know what you are going into with your eyes wide open. God's way is always clear. He does not hide His word from you. Jesus knew where He was going, what He was going to do.

John 14:3 KJV

"And if I go and prepare a place for you, I will come again, and receive you unto myself; that where I am, there ye may be also."

An agreement that does not specify what you are supposed to do from the beginning is a fraud. It is like a blind leading another blind.

Matthew 15:14 KJVA

"Let them alone: they be blind leaders of the blind. And if the blind lead the blind, both shall fall into the ditch."

God is not a spiritually blind leader. He sees clearly, so also should His children. We are not to be ignorant of the scheming of Satan. If you are already in the captivity of Satan by a swear, do not lose hope. What you need to do is pray to God for deliverance.

The First Book Of Adam and Eve Chap. LXXI (71):7- 9

7 Then God sent His Word unto Adam, who raised him up from where he lay, and said unto him, "O Adam, why hast thou sworn by My name, and why hast thou made agreement with Satan another time?"

8 But Adam wept, and said, "O God, forgive me, for I did this unwittingly; believing they were God's angels."

9 And God forgave Adam, saying, to him, "Beware of Satan."

- Repent and pray.

Micah 7:18-19 KJVA

"Be sorry for what you have done and ask God to forgive you of your wrong deed. He is a merciful God and does not want you destroyed.

19 "Who is a God like unto thee, that pardon iniquity, and pass by the transgression of the remnant of his heritage? He retain not his anger for ever, because he delights in mercy. He will turn again, he will have compassion upon us; he will subdue our iniquities; and thou wilt cast all their sins into the depths of the sea."

When you repent genuinely, He is ready to accept you back.

- Sin no more.

We are in the time of liberty in Christ. Liberty to follow God without compulsion. He wants us to follow Him voluntarily in His way of righteousness, but when we sin, we fall from His way.

Isaiah 59:1-3 KJVA

"Behold, the Lord 's hand is not shortened, that it cannot save; neither his ear heavy, that it cannot hear:

(2) but your iniquities have separated between you

and your God, and your sins have hid his face from you, that he will not hear.

(3) For your hands are defiled with blood, and your fingers with iniquity; your lips have spoken lies, your tongue hath muttered perverseness."

Sin separate us from God and brings us closer to Satan. When God delivers us from our fallen state, He wants us to toil in His path. That is why He gave us the law of liberty.

James 1:25 KJV
"But whoso look into the perfect law of liberty, and continue therein, he being not a forgetful hearer, but a doer of the work, this man shall be blessed in his deed."

Liberty does not give us freedom to sin, but freedom to do what God requires from us by our own will. We are required not to fall into sin by our own decision and not to put on the habit of falling into sin every now and then. If we keep falling into sin, do we know when we will have our last breath? The Bible says ...

Hebrews 9:27 KJV

"And as it is appointed unto men once to die, but after this the judgment:"

If you die while in your sinful state, Jesus Christ will condemn you with the devil and it will be nobody's fault but yours alone. Let us be weary of the spirit we let in, the advice we receive and the agreement we enter lest we fall into the devil's trap and sin unto God. Be vigilant and pray in accordance with the will of God, believing we are OVERCOMERS.

CHAPTER SEVEN
HURTFUL ADVICE

In a time of confusion, a period of indecision, man goes out of the way seeking for advice. As children of God, seeking for advice is not a bad thing, but accepting a compromising advice is bad. Any advice that put you against a fellow man, with a believer or non-believer, is evil. Advice that asks you to pay evil with evil, such advice is also evil.

Romans 12:17 ASV
"Render to no man evil for evil. Take thought for things honorable in the sight of all men."

An advice telling you to sideline one side is not from God and God's true child will not give such. Hurting someone is not God's way, it is the way of the devil.

The First Book Of Adam and Eve Chap. LXXVI (76):10-12.

10 But as to hard-hearted Cain, Satan came to him by night, showed himself and said unto him,

"Since Adam and Eve love thy brother Abel much more than they love thee, and wish to join him in marriage to thy beautiful sister, because they love him; but wish to join thee in marriage to his ill-favoured sister, because they hate thee;

11 "Now, therefore, I counsel thee, when they do that, to kill thy brother; then thy sister will be left for thee; and his sister will be cast, away."

12 And Satan departed from him. But the wicked One remained behind in the heart of Cain, who sought many a time, to kill his brother.

For an evil advice to penetrate the heart, you would have taught upon it, then the devil seized the opportunity to bring it to reality. Evil plan comes out of jealousy and insecurity of oneself. Jealousy brings hatred and hatred produced evil plan, an evil plan then leads to hurt or destruction of one's rival.

Proverbs 6:34 ASV

"For jealousy is the rage of a man; And he will not spare in the day of vengeance."

Hurtful advice will point out your shortcomings, laying the fault on someone else, giving you insecurity. You will then see a better person as your enemy, blaming the person for your predicament without you attempting to change your ways.

James 3:14-16 ASV

"But if ye have bitter jealousy and faction in your heart, glory not and lie not against the truth. This wisdom is not a wisdom that come down from above, but is earthly, sensual, devilish. For where jealousy and faction are, there is confusion and every vile deed."

The advice of Satan, with Cain's hidden taught germinated, and a plan was hatched.

The First Book Of Adam and Eve Chap. LXXVIII (78):6-11

6 Meanwhile Satan came to Cain in the figure of a man of the field, and said to him, "Behold Adam and Eve have taken counsel together about the marriage of you two; and they have agreed to marry Abel's sister to thee,

and thy sister to him.

7 "But if it was not that I love thee, I would not have told thee this thing. Yet if thou wilt take my advice, and hearken to me, I will bring: thee on thy wedding day beautiful robes, gold and silver in plenty, and my relations will attend thee."

8 Then Cain said with joy, "Where are thy relations?"

9 And Satan answered, "My relations are in a garden in the north, whither I once meant to bring thy father Adam; but he would not accept my offer.

10 "But thou, if thou wilt receive my words and if thou wilt come unto me after thy wedding, thou shalt rest from the misery in which thou art; and thou shalt rest and be better off than thy father Adam."

11 At these words of Satan Cain opened his ears, and leant towards his speech.

- Bribery comes from Satan.

Reward for a crime is bribery. Only an evil being will suggest that you hurt someone in return for a reward. Not all bribes will ask you to kill, but all will ask you to cover up a shortcoming in order to get a greater reward.

2 Samuel 13:1-5 ASV

"And it came to pass after this, that Absalom the son of David had a fair sister, whose name was Tamar; and Amnon the son of David loved her. And Amnon was so vexed that he fell sick because of his sister Tamar; for she was a virgin; and it seemed hard to Amnon to do anything unto her. But Amnon had a friend, whose name was Jonadab, the son of Shimeah, David's brother: and Jonadab was a very subtle man. And he said unto him, Why, O son of the king, art thou thus lean from day to day? wilt thou not tell me? And Amnon said unto him, I love Tamar, my brother Absalom's sister. And Jonadab said unto him, Lay thee down on thy bed, and feign thyself sick: and when thy father cometh to see thee, say unto him, Let my sister Tamar come, I pray thee, and give me bread to eat, and dress the food in my sight, that I may see it, and eat it from her hand."

His friend ill-advised him to perform a horrible act at the expense of his stepsister, not minding the disgrace and shame it will bring on his stepsister. What only consigned him was his wish and reward.

Also in the case of Absalom, King David's son ...

2 Samuel 17:1-4 AMP

"Then, Ahithophel said to Absalom, "Please let me choose 12,000 men, and I will set out and pursue David tonight. I will strike while he is weary and exhausted, and terrify him; and all the people with him will flee [in terror]. Then I will attack the king alone, and I will bring all the people [who follow David] back to you. The return of everyone depends on the [death of the] man you are seeking; then all the people will be at peace [and accept you as king]." So the plan pleased Absalom and all the elders of Israel."

Poor advice always sound pleasing and exciting. Ahithophel's advice sounded like the best to Absalom in paying back his father, for he was the king and failed to punish his stepbrother for hurting his sister. He wanted to get even with his father. Bribery and Shortcut walk together, both deceitful and it hurt at the long run. Hurting someone to be acceptable can never work.

Luke 9:51-54 ASV

"And it came to pass, when the days were well-nigh come that he should be received up, he stedfastly set his face to go to Jerusalem, and sent messengers before his face: and they went, and entered into a village of the

Samaritans, to make ready for him. And they did not receive him, because his face was as though he were going to Jerusalem. And when his disciples James and John saw this, they said, Lord, wilt thou that we bid fire to come down from heaven, and consume them?"

We do not force others to love us, rather; we love others to receive love in return.

1 Corinthians 13:4-5 AMP

"Love endures with patience and serenity, love is kind and thoughtful, and is not jealous or envious; love does not brag and is not proud or arrogant. It is not rude; it is not self-seeking, it is not provoked [nor overly sensitive and easily angered]; it does not take into account a wrong endured."

A selfish heart produces a heart of stone. It does not care for others and can be manipulated easily to do what is wrong, since it does not care for others' feelings.

- Pride gives room for misleading words.

Proverbs 16:18 AMP

"Pride goes before destruction, And a haughty spirit before a fall."

Pride in Cain gave access to Satan in his life. He wanted to be put in high esteem without him working to be a better person. He wanted to be regarded than every other person without him acknowledging others. What you dish out is what you get in return.

Matthew 7:12 AMP
"So then, in everything treat others the same way you want them to treat you, for this is [the essence of] the Law and the [writings of the] Prophets."

Do not expect others to respect and love you when you disrespect and despise them. You will only get what you give out. It is like a seed and a fruit. When you plant a wheat, be sure to harvest a bountiful wheat. But when you plant a stone, you reap nothing except a bare and hard sand starring you in the face.

Galatians 6:7 AMP
"Do not be deceived, God is not mocked [He will not allow Himself to be ridiculed, nor treated with contempt

nor allow His precepts to be scornfully set aside]; for whatever a man sows, this and this only is what he will reap."

Never forget that you will receive back everything you give. When you follow the hurtful advice of Satan, he will hurt you back, plus God's judgement on the wicked.

Overcoming wrong advice.
- Avoid ungodly company

Psalms 1:1 AMP

"Blessed [fortunate, prosperous, and favored by God] is the man who does not walk in the counsel of the wicked [following their advice and example], Nor stand in the path of sinners, Nor sit [down to rest] in the seat of scoffers (ridiculers)."

Mixing with the ungodly brings evil counsel. Children of the world can only offer their father's advice, which will go contrary to God's counsel.

John 8:44 AMP

"You are of your father the devil, and it is your will to

practice the desires [which are characteristic] of your father. He was a murderer from the beginning, and does not stand in the truth because there is no truth in him. When he lies, he speaks what is natural to him, for he is a liar and the father of lies and half-truths."

- Abhor no grudge.

Having a pure heart towards everyone brings peace.

Psalms 24:3-4 AMP

"Who may ascend onto the mountain of the LORD? And who may stand in His holy place? He who has clean hands and a pure heart, Who has not lifted up his soul to what is false, Nor has sworn [oaths] deceitfully."

When your heart is pure, it will be devoid of hatred. Satan can only deceive you when you have an unclean taught within you.

- Setting your mind on godly things

Romans 12:2 AMP

"And do not be conformed to this world [any longer with its superficial values and customs], but be transformed and progressively changed [as you mature spiritually] by the renewing of your mind [focusing on godly values and ethical attitudes], so that you may prove [for yourselves] what the will of God is, that which is good and acceptable and perfect [in His plan and purpose for you]."

Getting rid of evil thoughts and filling it with godly thoughts brings renewal of the spirit. It brings peace and happiness to oneself and to those around you.

- Study the word diligently.

To overcome the deceit of the devil and his schemes, you have to be familiar with the word of God.

Colossians 3:16 AMP

"Let the [spoken] word of Christ have its home within you [dwelling in your heart and mind—permeating every aspect of your being] as you teach [spiritual things] and admonish and train one another with all wisdom, singing psalms and hymns and spiritual songs with thankfulness in your hearts to God."

Wisdom of God preserves us from evil, it guides our

thoughts and ways. The word of God exposes the lies of Satan and upholds us with the truth. Fill your mind with love and the word of the Bible, the devil cannot overcome you with his hurtful advice. With good counsel from The Word, you are OVERCOMER.

CHAPTER EIGHT
SEXUAL DESIRE

The greatest and easiest fall Satan can bring to a minister of God is by arousing illicit sexual desire in him. In fact, eminent men on earth had fallen by their inability to control their sexual urge. Let us look at the wife of Potiphar and Joseph in the Bible.

Genesis 39:7-12 CSB

"After some time his master's wife looked longingly at Joseph and said, "Sleep with me." But he refused. "Look," he said to his master's wife, "with me here my master does not concern himself with anything in his house, and he has put all that he owns under my authority. No one in this house is greater than I am. He has withheld nothing from me except you, because you are his wife. So how could I do this immense evil, and how could I sin against God?" Although she spoke to Joseph day after day, he refused to go to bed with her. Now one day he went into the house to do his work, and none of the household servants were there. She grabbed him by his garment and said, "Sleep with me!" But leaving his garment in her hand, he escaped and ran outside."

The sexual urge in her weakened her spirit. It brought deceit to her, and she also wanted Joseph to fall for her deceit. Satan wanted Joseph to lose his place in the presence of God and cutting off the promise of God for his life.

Hebrews 13:4 CSB
"Marriage is to be honored by all and the marriage bed kept undefiled, because God will judge the sexually immoral and adulterers."

By having sexual intercourse with her, he would commit a great sin to Potiphar and God.

Second Book Of Adam and Eve Chap. III(3):4-8
4 Then Satan, the hater of all good, when he saw Adam thus alone, fasting and praying, appeared unto him in the form of a beautiful woman, who came and stood before him in the night of the fortieth day, and said unto him.
5 "O Adam, from the time ye have dwelt in this cave, we have experienced great peace from you, and your prayers have reached us, and we have been comforted about you.

6 "But now, O Adam, that thou hast gone up over the roof of the cave to sleep, we have had doubts about thee, and a great sorrow has come upon us because of thy separation from Eve. Then again, when thou art on the roof of this cave, thy prayer is poured out, and thy heart wanders from side to side.

7 "But when thou wast in the cave thy prayer was like fire gathered together; it came down to us, and thou didst find rest.

8 "Then I also grieved over thy children who are severed from thee; and my sorrow is great about the murder of thy son Abel; for he was righteous; and over a righteous man every one will grieve.

- False consigned

Satan appeared to Adam as this beautiful young woman to ignite the fire in him. He did not come to sympathize or come out of consigned, but to break his fast and stop his prayer. This will definitely annul all his forty days of prayer and fasting. All Adam's effort would have been wasted, and Satan also wanted Adam to sin to displease God.

Second Book of Adam and Eve Chap. III(3):9-10

9 "But I rejoiced over the birth of thy son Seth; yet after a little while I sorrowed greatly over Eve, because she is my sister. For when God sent a deep sleep over thee, and drew her out of

thy side, He brought me out also with her. But He raised her by placing her with thee, while He lowered me.

10 "I rejoiced over my sister for her being with thee. But God had made me a promise before, and said, 'Grieve not; when Adam has gone up on the roof of the Cave of Treasures, and is separated from Eve his wife, I will send thee to him, thou shalt join thyself to him in marriage, and bear him five children, as Eve did bear him five.'

Satan always brings confusion whenever he goes. He always lies. If God had created two women out of the rib of Adam, God would have told Adam. It was stated in...

Genesis 1:27 CSB

"So God created man in his own image; he created him in the image of God; he created them male and female."

Male and female He created them, not male and male or female male and females. God created one man and one woman. Her word was contrary to God's word, it was a word of deceit. She wanted to take the place of Eve, even though she claimed to be her sister. If she was truly consigned for her sister and was happy for her to have a family of her own, then why was she offering herself to Adam? She claimed to be better than Eve and will even bring forth better children.

Second Book of Adam and Eve Chap.III(3):11-14

11 "And now, lo! God's promise to me is fulfilled; for it is He who has sent me to thee for the wedding; because if thou wed me, I shall bear thee finer and better children than those of Eve.

12 "Then again, thou art as yet but a youth; end not thy youth in this world in sorrow; but spend the days of thy youth in mirth and pleasure. For thy days are few and thy trial is great. Be strong; end thy days in this world in rejoicing. I shall take pleasure in thee, and thou shall rejoice with me in this wise, and without fear.

13 "Up, then, and fulfil the command of thy God," she then drew near to Adam, and embraced him.

14 But when Adam saw that he should be overcome by her, he prayed to God with a fervent heart to deliver him from her.

- God's promise is always righteous.

God does not use defilement to fulfill His promise. Remember, God does not make mistakes.

The way of darkness leads to death, but the way of God is to live an eternal life. Seduction is a way of darkness. It may bring along a mouth watering offer, but it will end in destruction. God blessed King Solomon in wisdom and wealth, but his unable to withhold his sexual desire for women resulted in him marrying several women from ungodly nations, bringing his downfall.

1 Kings 11:1-4 CSB

"King Solomon loved many foreign women in addition to Pharaoh's daughter: Moabite, Ammonite, Edomite, Sidonian, and Hittite women from the nations about which the Lord had told the Israelites,

"You must not intermarry with them, and they must not intermarry with you, because they will turn your heart away to follow their gods."

To these women Solomon was deeply attached in love. He had seven hundred wives who were princesses and three hundred who were concubines, and they turned his heart away.

When Solomon was old, his wives turned his heart away to follow other gods. He was not wholeheartedly devoted to the Lord his God, as his father David had been."

Overcoming illicit sexual desire

- Uncontrolled sexual desire is an immorality in the sight of God, it defiles the body.

1 Corinthians 6:18-20 CSB

"Flee sexual immorality! Every other sin a person commits is outside the body, but the person who is sexually immoral sins against his own body. Don't you know that your body is the temple of the Holy Spirit who is in you, whom you have from

God? You are not your own, for you were bought at a price. So glorify God with your body."

Keep your body under control because your body is meant to glorify God.

- Renew your spirit daily.

Galatians 5:16 CSB
"I say, then, walk by the Spirit and you will certainly not carry out the desire of the flesh."

Devil arouses sexual desire in man to corrupt the spirit when the spirit is weak. Continual renewal of the spirit will strengthen your spirit and keep your body under control and holy.

Romans 12:2 CSB
"Do not be conformed to this age, but be transformed by the renewing of your mind, so that you may discern what is the good, pleasing, and perfect will of God."

Whatever goes to the spirit comes from your mind, so fill your and spirit with the things of God. This will always keep you inline.

- **Prayer without ceasing.**

Pray constantly, for the spirit is willing, but the flesh is weak. But with prayer, we will overcome the lust of flesh and of eyes.

1 Thessalonians 5:16-18 CSB

"Rejoice always, pray constantly, give thanks in everything; for this is God's will for you in Christ Jesus."

By continuous prayer, controlling our sexual urge and meditating on the word of God. We will continue to be OVERCOMERS.

CHAPTER NINE
SECRECY

Ephesians 5:11-12 KJV

"And have no fellowship with the unfruitful works of darkness, but rather reprove them. For it is a shame even to speak of those things which are done of them in secret."

Secrecy is a deceit brought by the devil to deceive man. It is an offer from Satan to make a better deal with us if only we can hide it from family, friends and good people around us. Most people addicted to drugs today got it from their secret use of drug. Pedophilias carry out evil plan in secret, bribery is done in secret, everything that can bring shame, humiliation and punishment are always done in secret. Unfortunately, a forbidding fruit is always enticing.

Proverbs 9:17 KJV

"Stolen waters are sweet, and bread eaten in secret is pleasant."

Satan uses this tool to bring us closer to him and separate us from God. Secrecy and darkness are one. Secrecy is hiding your act while darkness is hiding in the dark.

Second Book Of Adam and Eve Chap. V (5):1-4

AS for Seth, when he was seven years old, he knew good and evil, and was consistent in fasting and praying, and spent all his nights in entreating God for mercy and forgiveness.

2 He also fasted when bringing up his offering every day, more than his father did; for he was of a fair countenance, like unto an angel of God. He also had a good heart, preserved the finest qualities of his soul: and for this reason he brought up his offering every day.

3 And God was pleased with his offering; but He was also pleased with his purity. And he continued thus in doing the will of God, and of his father and mother, until he was seven years old.

4 After that, as he was coming down from the altar, having ended his offering, Satan appeared unto him in the form of a beautiful angel, brilliant with light; with a staff of light in his hand, himself girt about with a girdle of light.

When Satan could not overpower Adam, so he went for his son, Seth. Seth was pure in heart, righteous and obedient to his parents, but Satan, the hater of good things, was not pleased with the relationship Seth shared with God. Satan brought another scheme of enticing with secrecy. Before secrecy can come from Satan, we first must have put forth some strategies.

Second Book Of Adam and Eve Chap. V(5):5-11

5 He greeted Seth with a beautiful smile, and began to beguile him with fair words, saying to him, "O Seth, why abidest thou in this mountain? For it is rough, full of stones and of sand, and of trees with no good fruit on them; a wilderness without habitations and without towns; no good place to dwell in. But all is heat, weariness, and trouble."

6 He said further, "But we dwell in beautiful places, in another world than this earth. Our world is one of light and our condition is of the best; our women are handsomer

than any others; and I wish thee, O Seth, to wed one of them; because I see that thou art fair to look upon, and in this land there is not one woman good enough for thee. Besides, all those who live in this world, are only five souls.

7 "But in our world there are very many men and many maidens, all more beautiful one than another. I wish, therefore, to remove thee hence, that thou mayest see my relations and be wedded to which ever thou likest.

8 "Thou shalt then abide by me and be at peace; thou shalt be filled with splendour and light, as we are.

9 "Thou shalt remain in our world. and rest from this world and the misery of it; thou shalt never again feel faint and weary;

thou shalt never bring up an offering, nor sue for mercy; for thou shalt commit no more sin, nor be swayed by passions.

10 "And if thou wilt hearken to what I say, thou shalt wed one of my daughters; for with us it is no sin so to do; neither is it reckoned animal lust.

11 "For in our world we have no God; but we all are gods; we all are of the light, heavenly, powerful, strong and glorious."

- Satan brings ridicule

For a man to leave his current position, he is displeased with that position, surrounding, circumstances, and people around him. Satan knows this very well, so he uses it in deceiving man.

- Shows the unpleasant form

Satan will point out the unpleasant part to you for you to hate it all. He will point to show how difficult, stressful, underpaid, time-consuming and unpopular that thing you have is. For a minister in a new church, rural area, smaller congregation or in an unfriendly country, Satan will point out all the unpleasantness to you, making you to hate the calling, ministry, the people, the area, then despise the gospel at last.

- Entrance to another world

Satan tried to show Seth another world different from God's. Likewise, Satan has shown several ministers ways that were different to God's way. Ways of luxury, popularity, diabolic fast ways to signs and wonders, prosperity gospel in place of salvation message.

- Atheism

Satan turns the heart of man against God by the

belief that we are gods by ourselves and we do not need God the Almighty.

Denial of God sprang up because of the spirit of pride in man. When God blesses a man to a certain stage, Satan will introduce a self-dependent spirit to that person and if you are weak in spirit, if you have gone astray or if you do not fellowship constantly with God, you will believe that you are god yourself.

You will begin to believe that everything you achieve come about by your own power and intelligence. You will begin to regard yourself more and disregard God the Almighty. People will begin to shower you with accolade bringing you to a self-immortality. You then begin to look at every other person as inferior and yourself as the ultimate.

Jeremiah 9:22-23 KJV

"Speak, Thus saith the Lord, Even the carcasses of men shall fall as dung upon the open field, and as the handful after the harvestman, and none shall gather them. Thus saith the Lord, Let not the wise man glory in his wisdom, neither let the mighty man glory in his might, let not the rich man glory in his riches:"

Satan knew Seth was in good standing with God, so he introduced secrecy to him.

Second Book Of Adam and Eve Chap. VI(6):5-7

5 Again Seth said, "I am afraid of doing any thing without my father's and mother's leave, lest I perish like my brother Cain, and like my father Adam, who transgressed the commandment of God. But, behold, thou knowest this place; come, and meet me here to-morrow."

6 When Satan heard this, he said to Seth, "If thou tellest thy father Adam what I have told thee, he will not let thee come with me.

7 But hearken to me; do not tell thy father and mother what I have said to thee; but come with me to-day, to our world; where thou shalt see beautiful things and enjoy thyself there, and revel this day among my children, beholding them and taking thy fill of mirth; and rejoice ever more. Then I shall bring thee back to this place to-morrow; but if thou wouldest rather abide with me, so be it."

- Secrecy brings hurt to loved ones.

By keeping secret from people close to you, you are indirectly hurting them.

The Spirit of God can not tell you to do things irrationally without consideration of the impact it will have on people around you.

Second Book Of Adam and Eve Chap. VI(6):8-11

8 Then Seth answered, "The spirit of my father and of my mother, hangs on me; and if I hide from them one day, they will die, and God will hold me guilty of sinning against them.

9 "And except that they know I am come to this place to bring up to it my offering, they would not be separated from me one hour; neither should I go to any other place, unless they let me. But they treat me most kindly, because I come back to them quickly."

10 Then Satan said to him, "What will happen to thee if thou hide thyself from them one night, and return to them at break of day?"

11 But Seth, when he saw how he kept on talking, and that he would not leave him-ran, and went up to the altar, and spread his hands unto God, and sought deliverance from Him.

- Paying evil for good.

The spirit of darkness only knows how to be bad. The

Spirit Of God will never pay evil for a good deed because that would go against God's rule.

Proverbs 17:13 KJV

"Whoso rewardeth evil for good, evil shall not depart from his house."

Paying evil for good comes from evil, itself which is the devil.

- Confrontational

Any spirit that becomes confrontational is from the devil. The Spirit of God is calm.

Matthew 11:29 KJV

"Take my yoke upon you, and learn of me; for I am meek and lowly in heart: and ye shall find rest unto your souls."

Jesus does not force himself on anybody. God's way is a path of freedom to fellowship. Any spirit that threatens is not of God and must be cast away.

Overcoming deceit of secrecy.

- Wisdom

Be full of wisdom of God.

James 1:5 KJV

"If any of you lack wisdom, let him ask of God, that give to all men liberally, and upbraid not; and it shall be given him."

It is by the wisdom of God we can be able to defeat the scheming of the devil and loose ourselves from his web.

- Confirmation from God

Second Book Of Adam and Eve Chap. VI(6):3-4

3 But Seth said to him, "Thy speech has amazed me; and thy beautiful description of it all.

4 "Yet I cannot go with thee to-day; not until I have gone to my father Adam and to my mother Eve, and told them all thou hast said to me. Then if they give me leave to go with thee, I will come."

Confirm any idea, advice, or spiritual messages giving to you from God before going with it. The devil is very cunning and wise deceitfully. We must be extra careful with him. He is not a man, but a spirit, the king of darkness.

Ephesians 6:12 KJV

"For we wrestle not against flesh and blood, but against principalities, against powers, against the rulers of the darkness of this world, against spiritual wickedness in high places."

Satan knows the act of manipulation, so we must be alert to everything we do. Only through the confirmation of God can we know to do the right thing and follow the right way.

Living rightly makes us OVERCOMERS.

CHAPTER TEN
RE-INCARNATION

The word of God says,

Hebrews 9:27 KJV

"And as it is appointed unto men once to die, but after this the judgment:"

We should not be ignorant of the devil's scheming, neither should we be far away from the world of God. Every dead person has come to the end of his journey on earth. He is waiting for the judgment of his deeds on earth, waiting for his reward, either good or bad. God does not minister to us through the dead.

1 Chronicles 10:13 KJV

"So Saul died for his transgression which he committed against the Lord, even against the word of the Lord, which he kept not, and also for asking counsel of one that had a familiar spirit, to enquire of it."

The Comforter is with us now to show us all things, but the devil still deceives some by acting as a late loved one. In this chapter, we shall look at how Satan lures the righteous to sin, lured to the world and call to ministry broken.

Jared was the head of his people. He was in charge, praying to God and instructing the children of Adam on righteous living. But suddenly he was lured away.

Second Book Of Adam and Eve Chap. XVII(17):4-10

4 Satan then appeared to him with thirty men of his hosts, in the form of handsome men; Satan himself being the elder and tallest among them, with a fine beard.

5 They stood at the mouth of the cave, and called out Jared, from within it.

6 He came out to them, and found them looking like fine men, full of light, and of great beauty. He wondered at their beauty and at their looks; and thought within himself whether they might not be of the children of Cain.

7 He said also in his heart, "As the children of Cain cannot come up to the height of this mountain, and none of them is so handsome as these appear to be; and among these men there is not one of my kindred--they must be strangers."

8 Then Jared and they exchanged a greeting and he said to the elder among them, "O my father, explain to me the wonder

that is in thee, and tell me who these are, with thee; for they look to me like strange men."

9 Then the elder began to weep, and the rest wept with him; and he said to Jared: "I am Adam whom God made first; and this is Abel my son, who was killed by his brother Cain, into whose heart Satan put to murder him.

10 "Then this is my son Seth, whom I asked of the Lord, who gave him to me, to comfort me instead of Abel.

He knew perfectly well that the children of Cain can not come up the mountain and he was also aware of the promise of God to bring them back after 5,500 years, still he went out to inquire who these people are. He can feel the strangeness in them just like we feel it in our spirit when a contrary spirit is at work, but most times we choose to be curious. The corpses of his ancestors were in the cave. Then how do these have earthly bodies?

Second Book Of Adam and Eve Chap. XVII(17):13-22

13 Then the elder said to him, "Marvel not, O my son; we live in the land north of the garden, which God created before the world. He would not let us live there, but placed us inside the garden, below which ye are now dwelling.

14 "But after that I transgressed, He made me come out of it, and I was left to dwell in this cave; great and sore troubles came upon me; and when my death drew near, I commanded my

son Seth to tend his people well; and this my commandment is to be handed from one to another, unto the end of the generations to come.

15 "But, O Jared, my son, we live in beautiful regions, while you live here in misery, as this thy father Mahalaleel informed me; telling me that a great flood will come and overwhelm the whole earth.

16 "Therefore, O my son, fearing for your sakes, I rose and took my children with me, and came hither for us to visit thee and thy children; but I found thee standing in this cave weeping, and thy children scattered about this mountain, in the heat and in misery.

17 "But, O my son, as we missed our way, and came as far as this, we found other men below this mountain; who inhabit a beautiful country, full of trees and of fruits, and of all manner of verdure; it is like a garden; so that when we found them we thought they were you; until thy father Mahalaleel told me they were no such thing.

18 "Now, therefore, O my son, hearken to my counsel, and go down to them, thou and thy children. Ye will rest from all this suffering in which ye are. But if thou wilt not go down to them, then, arise, take thy children, and come with us to our garden; ye shall live in our beautiful land, and ye shall rest from all this trouble, which thou and thy children are now bearing."

19 But Jared when he heard this discourse from the elder, wondered; and went hither and thither, but at that moment he

found not one of his children.

20 Then he answered and said to the elder, "Why have you hidden yourselves until this day?"

21 And the elder replied, "If thy father had not told us, we should not have known it."

22 Then Jared believed his words were true.

For any re-incarnated body, the devil and his host can only imbed it. Re-incarnation is to mislead man from God. It will take some features of the late with a make-believe of a wider being. These ancestors claimed to come from a better world, but yet they can not help themselves by doing what they proposed to someone else. In the case of Jared, they came from a different and better world than this, our world, know more and nothing can go wrong with them, yet they missed their way. They knew that the world was ending, yet they wanted the holy children to go down and mix with the children of Cain, the immoral sect. If they were their ancestors truly, they would not want them to fall into sin as they fell. They claimed that by death; they are now in a better place. Why then were they against godly living instead of praising them for following their instructions? Just like Jared fell for the sweet words, many ministers have fallen to such fine words of deceit. It has made many to abandon God's way to follow a make-believe better way only to realize that they have been duped.

Mark 8:36 KJV

"For what shall it profit a man, if he shall gain the whole world, and lose his own soul?"

Many perceive deceit of the devil in his dealing, but our curiosity gets the better of us.

James 1:14-15 KJV

"But every man is tempted, when he is drawn away of his own lust, and enticed. Then when lust hath conceived, it bringeth forth sin: and sin, when it is finished, bringeth forth death."

Overcoming deceit of re-incarnation.

- Be cautious

We must be extra careful about what we are digging into lest we get trapped in the bondage of Satan.

1 Peter 1:14 AMP

"[Live] as obedient children [of God]; do not be conformed to the evil desires which governed you in your ignorance [before you knew the requirements and transforming power of the good news regarding salvation]."

- Stay away from spiritism.

Spiritism involves invoking unconventional spirit, angels of

God do not answer to invocation. When you invoke, you get the host of darkness into action, pretending to be angels of God or someone familiar to you.

Leviticus 19:31 AMP "'Do not turn to mediums [who pretend to consult the dead] or to spiritists [who have spirits of divination]; do not seek them out to be defiled by them. I am the LORD your God."

- Look to God for guidance

John 16:13 KJV

"Howbeit when he, the Spirit of truth, is come, he will guide you into all truth: for he shall not speak of himself; but whatsoever he shall hear, that shall he speak: and he will shew you things to come."

The Holy Spirit is there to guide you, reveal the unknown to you, and discern every spirit for you. Only with the Holy Spirit can you withstand the deceit of the devil. If you are yet to receive the Holy Spirit, do that now. Call on Him to abide in your life. Invite Him into your life to teach you all things. Holy Spirit is the promise from the Father to a believer.

John 14:26 KJV

"But the Comforter, which is the Holy Ghost, whom the

Father will send in my name, he shall teach you all things, and bring all things to your remembrance, whatsoever I have said unto you."

Get closer to God, walk with the Holy Spirit and give the word of God a place in your heart. God the Father, Son and Holy Spirit will empower you and you will become an OVERCOMER.

CHAPTER ELEVEN
UNGODLY FELLOWSHIP

1 Corinthians 15:33 KJV

"Be not deceived: evil communications corrupt good manners."

Union with unbelievers mostly resulted in backsliding. We forget to take our stand, to distance ourselves from their act, but we take part in what they do, how they live their lives, their ideologies and philosophy. Their way of lives later becomes ours, forgetting we are children of the Most High.

2 Corinthians 6:14 KJV

"Be ye not unequally yoked together with unbelievers: for what fellowship hath righteousness with unrighteousness? and what communion hath light with darkness?"

Unfortunately, believers' children now find non-believers attractive than that brother or sister in the church. We now tag our godly fellows dull, who do not have a life. We now find a minister to be too plain, void of excitement.

Esau, the son of Isaac, was married to women from people God despised because of their idolatry. This termed him as disobedient, he did not care if God is happy with him or not; he did not even seek his parents' approval before getting involved with those idolatry women. He got to know about the displeasure his wives brought on his parents after he had already married them.

Genesis 26:34-35 KJV

"And Esau was forty years old when he took to wife Judith the daughter of Beeri the Hittite, and Bashemath the daughter of Elon the Hittite: Which were a grief of mind unto Isaac and to Rebekah."

We should not forget Samson, the mighty warrior who fought and won many battles single-handedly. Sadly, he was later captured by his lust for strange company.

Judges 14:1-3 AMP

"Samson went down to Timnah and at Timnah he saw a woman, one of the daughters of the Philistines.

So he went back and told his father and his mother, "I saw a woman in Timnah, one of the daughters of the Philistines; now get her for me as a wife."

But his father and mother said to him, "Is there no woman among the daughters of your relatives, or among all our people, that you must go to take a wife from the uncircumcised (pagan) Philistines?"

And Samson said to his father, "Get her for me, because she looks pleasing to me.""

He preferred strange and immoral women to known, upright and sane woman. He loved to explore the unthinkable and the outcast of God. Its end was betrayal, captivity, torment and destruction.

Let us look at the children of Seth on the mountain.

Second Book Of Adam and Eve Chap. XX(20):12-16

12 But when the children of Seth heard the noise, they wondered, and came by companies, and stood on the top of the mountain to look at those below; and they did thus a whole year.

13 When, at the end of that year, Genun saw that they were being won over to him little by little, Satan entered into him, and taught him to make dyeing-stuffs for garments of divers patterns, and made him understand how to dye crimson and purple and what not.

14 And the sons of Cain who wrought all this, and shone in beauty and gorgeous apparel, gathered together at the foot of the mountain in splendour, with horns and gorgeous dresses, and horse races, committing all manner of abominations.

15 Meanwhile the children of Seth, who were on the Holy Mountain, prayed and praised God, in the place of the hosts of angels who had fallen; wherefore God had called them "angels," because He rejoiced over them greatly.

16 But after this, they no longer kept His commandment, nor held by the promise He had made to their fathers; but they relaxed from their fasting and praying, and from the counsel of Jared their father. And they kept on gathering together on the top of the mountain, to look upon the children of Cain, from morning until evening, and upon what they did, upon their beautiful dresses and ornaments.

Most times we claimed to be free of sin, forgetting that by looking and longing, by dreaming up in our heart things of the world, we are gradually sinning and defiling ourselves and our spirit. Lusts of the eyes have defiled many ministers.

Matthew 5:27-29 AMP

"You have heard that it was said, 'YOU SHALL NOT COMMIT ADULTERY'; but I say to you that everyone who [so much as] looks at a woman with lust for her has already committed adultery with her in his heart. If your right eye makes you stumble and leads you to sin, tear it out and throw it away [that is, remove yourself from the source of temptation]; for it is better for you to lose one of the parts of your body, than for your whole body to be thrown into hell."

They may not have the courage to carry out their secret wants for the fear of people's reaction. Fear of the judgment of people is greater than the judgment of God.

Matthew 10:28 KJV
"And fear not them which kill the body, but are not able to kill the soul: but rather fear him which is able to destroy both soul and body in hell."

The children of Seth in their heart have already derailed. They were still on the mountain for the fear of the unknown, sacred of what they may see and not wanting to lose their place on the mountain. Many ministers wish to be in the world, to enjoy all the benefits of the ungodly, live lives recklessly, get into unlawful sexual act but they fear been recognized as a sinner, unwilling to lose the position in ministry. Even though their hearts are no more in what they do and where they are. Indirectly, they are no more part of the ministry of Jesus, only by titles of offices they are called.

Matthew 7:21-23 KJV
"Not every one that saith unto me, Lord, Lord, shall enter into the kingdom of heaven; but he that doeth the will of my Father which is in heaven. Many will say to me in that day, Lord, Lord, have we not prophesied in thy name? and in thy name

have cast out devils? and in thy name done many wonderful works? And then will I profess unto them, I never knew you: depart from me, ye that work iniquity."

When a thought already formed in the mind, Satan will build it up. He uses a seed of worldliness to manipulate man, making man to fall into bigger sin.

Second Book Of Adam and Eve Chap. XX(20):17-24

17 Then the children of Cain looked up from below, and saw the children of Seth, standing in troops on the top of the mountain; and they called to them to come down to them.

18 But the children of Seth said to them from above, "We don't know the way." Then Genun, the son of Lamech, heard them say they did not know the way, and he bethought himself how he might bring them down.

19 Then Satan appeared to him by night, saying, "There is no way for them to come down from the mountain on which they dwell; but when they come to-morrow, say to them, 'Come ye to the western side of the mountain; there you will find the way of a stream of water, that comes down to the foot of the mountain, between two hills; come down that way to us.'"

20 Then when it was day, Genun blew the horns and beat the drums below the mountain, as he was wont. The children of Seth heard it, and came as they used to do.

21 Then Genun said to them from down below, "Go to the

western side of the mountain, there you will find the way to come down."

22 But when the children of Seth heard these words from him, they went back into the cave to Jared, to tell him all they had heard.

23 Then when Jared heard it, he was grieved; for he knew that they would transgress his counsel.

24 After this a hundred men of the children of Seth gathered together, and said among themselves, "Come, let us go down to the children of Cain, and see what they do, and enjoy ourselves with them."

Satan draws man little by little into sin. Before you know it, you are already deep in sin.

- **Direction from Satan.**

The children of Cain offered them fellowship with how to enter into their ungodly fold.

Many ministers were regenerated and were undefiled by sin, but the company they kept resulted in their defilement. Children of ministers go astray because of lack of discipline and admonishment, lack of self-control, and the belief of having a permanent intercessor for them who will always stand in between, should God be angry.

1 Samuel 2:12-17 AMP

"The sons of Eli [Hophni and Phinehas] were worthless (dishonorable, unprincipled) men; they did not know [nor respect] the LORD and the custom of the priests with [the sacrifices of] the people. When any man was offering a sacrifice, the priest's servant would come while the meat was boiling, with a three-pronged [meat] fork in his hand; then he would thrust it into the pan, or kettle, or caldron, or pot; everything that the fork brought up the priest would take for himself. This is what they did in Shiloh to all [the sacrifices of] the Israelites who came there. Also, before they burned (offered) the fat, the priest's servant would come and say to the man who was sacrificing, "Give the priest meat to roast, since he will not accept boiled meat from you, only raw." If the man said to him, " Certainly they are to burn (offer) the fat first, and then you may take as much as you want," then the priest's servant would say, "No! You shall give it to me now or I will take it by force." So the sin of the [two] young men [Hophni and Phinehas] was very great before the LORD, for the men treated the offering of the LORD disrespectfully."

The children of Eli knew they were in the wrong. Their father knew how his sons were acting against the law of God, yet he did not discipline them. Yes, the Bible says he warned them, but warning differs from discipline. He could have suspended or expelled them from the sanctuary, cutting off benefits they receive from the office, make them serve punishment. But he let them go on, living their lives to the fullest, ruining other people's lives.

Hebrews 10:30-31 AMP

"For we know Him who said, "VENGEANCE IS M INE [retribution and the deliverance of justice rest with Me], I WILL REPAY [the wrongdoer]." And again, "THE LORD WILL JUDGE HIS PEOPLE." It is a fearful and terrifying thing to fall into the hands of the living God [incurring His judgment and wrath]."

God will surely judge everyone according to his work and in God's judgment, there is no partiality.

Romans 2:11 AMP

"For God shows no partiality [no arbitrary favoritism; with Him one person is not more important than another]."

Satan uses our privilege of fellowship with God to bring out pride in Ministers' children. Over-familiarity with God by ministers brings disregard to God's law. Some ministers believe they are over-special, someone too important to God, a vessel God must need before carrying out His work.

Ephesians 2:8-10 AMP

"For it is by grace [God's remarkable compassion and favor drawing you to Christ] that you have been saved [actually delivered from judgment and given eternal life] through faith. And this [salvation] is not of yourselves [not through your own effort], but it is the [undeserved, gracious] gift of God; not as a result of [your] works [nor your attempts to keep the Law], so that no one will [be able to] boast or take credit in any way [for his salvation]. For we are His workmanship [His own master work, a work of art], created in Christ Jesus [reborn from above—spiritually transformed, renewed, ready to be used] for good works, which God prepared [for us] beforehand [taking paths which He set], so that we would walk in them [living the good life which He prearranged and made ready for us]."

God does not need anyone to be God. Before man's existence, God was existing. Before the earth He was, before calling us into His ministry, His ministry has been there, He has been working before God created man, we only receive grace to be part of His Kingdom.

Second Book Of Adam and Eve Chap. XX(20):32-33

32 Then Satan made them look most beautiful before the sons of Seth, as he also made the sons of Seth appear of the fairest in the eyes of the daughters of Cain, so that the daughters of Cain lusted after the sons of Seth like ravenous beasts, and the sons of Seth after the daughters of Cain, until they committed abomination with them.

33 But after they had thus fallen into this defilement, they

returned by the way they had come, and tried to ascend the Holy Mountain. But they could not, because the stones of that holy mountain were of fire flashing before them, by reason of which they could not go up again.

- **None is irreplaceable**

The children of Seth thought they were irreplaceable, someone who could come as wished.

God is Self-Existence and Self-Sufficient. Man needs God to live, also we need Him to survive. It is through God's work we survive daily. If God cut off air from the earth for just five minutes, unimaginable things will happen to humans. No one should think of himself as the Almighty. Never think none is like you because man is not God. We are only to share in His attributes and minister in His government. A governor can never be more powerful than the President. Just like the children of Seth went astray thinking they could find their way back to God, so have many ministers gone astray intentionally, thinking they can bribe their way back to God. They intended to use emotional blackmail in coming back to God.

Hebrews 6:4-6 AMP

"For [it is impossible to restore to repentance] those who have once been enlightened [spiritually] and who have tasted and consciously experienced the heavenly gift and have shared in the Holy Spirit, and have tasted and consciously experienced the good word of God and the powers of the age (world) to come, and then have fallen away—it is impossible to bring them back again to repentance, since they again nail the Son of God on the cross [for as far as they are concerned, they are treating the death of Christ as if they were not saved by it], and are holding Him up again to public disgrace."

It is easy for an ardent sinner to be called into the fold of God, for he does not know what he is doing and has not received light than an anointed to fall and be called back into the fold for he makes rubbish of his office except for some selected few that receive grace.

Lastly, getting dirty to be clean is a deceit of the devil. Some children of God went astray in order to bring back their fellow, who fell into sin.

Second Book Of Adam and Eve Chap. XXI(21):1
AFTER this another company gathered together, and they went to look after their brethren; but they perished as well as they. And so it was, company after company, until only a few of them were left.

Falling into sin for the sake of the gospel is against God's will. He never wants us to dine with the devil in order to loose souls from the shackles of Satan. No one gets dirty to make clean.

Romans 12:1-2 CSB "Therefore, brothers and sisters, in view of the mercies of God, I urge you to present your bodies as a living sacrifice, holy and pleasing to God; this is your true worship. Do not be conformed to this age, but be transformed by the renewing of your mind, so that you may discern what is the good, pleasing, and perfect will of God."

The word of God urges us to fight evil with good, not to exchange good for evil. We are not to leave our godly lives to save the lost hence, we get lost in the process.

Colossians 3:2 KJV "Set your affection on things above, not on things on the earth."

Overcoming ungodly fellowship
I are enjoin to deal with everybody equally, show love to everyone but not to behave like everyone.

Romans 12:2 KJV "And be not conformed to this world: but be ye transformed by the renewing of your mind, that ye may prove what is that good, and acceptable, and perfect, will of God."

Our ways are to be light for the fallen, showing them the way and not the other way round.

Matthew 5:16 KJV

"Let your light so shine before men, that they may see your good works, and glorify your Father which is in heaven."

We are not to quench our light to enter darkness, but to ignite our fire for the darkness to see a path bringing them outside of darkness. While proclaiming the gospel, on no account should we let our guide down lest we fall.

By the continual fellowship with God The Father, Son and Holy Spirit, we will remain OVERCOMERS.

CHAPTER TWELVE
EMERGENCE OF OVERCOMER

Looking back at all forms of deceit Satan uses in misleading man, we realize that is difficult to sail through all. We need God to survive, so I will take us through some steps to take to become overcomers.

1 John 5:5 KJV
"Who is he that overcome the world, but he that believe that Jesus is the Son of God?"

- Sanctification

Our father's disobedience brought sin to our lives, which the devil uses as a channel to gain access to our lives. Through the grace of God, we receive the salvation of Christ, but as a man whose flesh is weak, we sin against our wish.

Romans 7:15-20 AMP
"For I do not understand my own actions [I am baffled and bewildered by them]. I do not practice what I want to do, but I am doing the very thing I hate [and yielding to my human nature,

my worldliness—my sinful capacity]. Now if I habitually do what I do not want to do, [that means] I agree with the Law, confessing that it is good (morally excellent). So now [if that is the case, then] it is no longer I who do it [the disobedient thing which I despise], but the sin [nature] which lives in me. For I know that nothing good lives in me, that is, in my flesh [my human nature, my worldliness—my sinful capacity]. For the willingness [to do good] is present in me, but the doing of good is not. For the good that I want to do, I do not do, but I practice the very evil that I do not want. But if I am doing the very thing I do not want to do, I am no longer the one doing it [that is, it is not me that acts], but the sin [nature] which lives in me."

We wish to be pure in heart and soul, but the flesh always falls for the devil. Then we need God's sanctification to purge us from our sins.

Psalms 51:2 AMP
"Wash me thoroughly from my wickedness and guilt And cleanse me from my sin."

By sanctification of our mind with the blood of Jesus, we will become clean.

Matthew 26:28 AMP
"For this is My blood of the [new and better] covenant,

which [ratifies the agreement and] is being poured out for many [as a substitutionary atonement] for the forgiveness of sins."

With the blood of Jesus we are clean, free from sin and Satan, free from flesh.

- Daily renewal of the spirit

John 4:24 KJV
"God is a Spirit: and they that worship him must worship him in spirit and in truth."

After the blood has sanctified us, for the fruit of the flesh to die and the fruit of the Spirit to manifest, we need the daily feeding. Daily feeding of the spirit is by reading His word; the Holy Bible. That is where you get the undiluted word of God. It will guide and open your understanding of His Being. Reading of the word of God constantly brings you to the knowledge of God. Remember, you are to practice what you read. God requires from slums to be doers of the word and not just the hearers.

James 1:22-24 AMP
"But prove yourselves doers of the word [actively and continually obeying God's precepts], and not merely listeners [who hear the word but fail to internalize its meaning], deluding yourselves [by unsound reasoning contrary to the truth]. For if

anyone only listens to the word without obeying it, he is like a man who looks very carefully at his natural face in a mirror; for once he has looked at himself and gone away, he immediately forgets what he looked like."

Obedient is by action, while listening is for remembrance. But when we hear and do, listen and obey, then we will emerge as overcomers.

- **Work inline with the Spirit.**

Overcoming the darkness is not a onetime battle. It is continuous; you defeat a form another comes. So you need the Holy Spirit at all times.

Matthew 12:43-45 KJV

"When the unclean spirit is gone out of a man, he walk through dry places, seeking rest, and find none. Then he saith, I will return into my house from whence I came out; and when he is come, he findeth it empty, swept, and garnished. Then goeth he, and taketh with himself seven other spirits more wicked than himself, and they enter in and dwell there: and the last state of that man is worse than the first. Even so shall it be also unto this wicked generation."

The Holy Spirit is the one to guide against evil spirits and their deceit. But you have to walk in accordance with the Holy

Spirit in these ways:

- Humility

James 4:6 AMP

"But He gives us more and more grace [through the power of the Holy Spirit to defy sin and live an obedient life that reflects both our faith and our gratitude for our salvation]. Therefore, it says, "GOD IS OPPOSED TO THE PROUD and HAUGHTY, BUT [continually] GIVES [the gift of] GRACE TO THE HUMBLE [who turn away from self-righteousness].""

A child of God must be humble at all times. Your anointing as a minister does not give you the permission to be boastful or disrespectful to people. Jesus expect a servant leadership from us.

John 13:12-16 AMP

"So when He had washed their feet and put on His [outer] robe and reclined at the table again, He said to them, "Do you understand what I have done for you? You call Me Teacher and Lord, and you are right in doing so, for that is who I am. So if I, the Lord and the Teacher, washed your feet, you ought to wash one another's feet as well. For I gave you [this as] an example, so that you should do [in turn] as I did to you. I assure you and most solemnly say to you, a slave is not greater than his master, nor is one who is sent greater than the one who sent him."

Jesus Christ never humiliated his disciples, he never rubbish his followers, neither did he make mockery of their state. He taught in humility and respect. Any minister who wants to keep his position in the vineyard must be ready to be humble and respectful of everyone.

- Love all

God is love, and He wants that from His children. The law of love supersedes all other laws.

Mark 12:30-31 AMP

"And you shall love the lord your god with all your heart, and with all your soul (life), and with all your mind (thought, understanding), and with all your strength.' This is the second: 'you shall [unselfishly] love your neighbor as yourself.' There is no other commandment greater than these."

When you love God, you will love His works, calling, His people, His words. You will want nothing to go wrong in His vineyard. You will become a good shepherd, always looking after His sheep. If you truly love God, you will feed the sheep spiritually, materially, morally, and with your goods. You will not only be consigned with getting tithes from them, but you will give from what you have. You will not compel them to give you, but you will bring out their giving side with your love, just like the Apostle Paul did to the church of God.

2 Corinthians 8:1-5 AMP

"Now, brothers and sisters, we want to tell you about the grace of God which has been evident in the churches of Macedonia [awakening in them a longing to contribute]; for during an ordeal of severe distress, their abundant joy and their deep poverty [together] overflowed in the wealth of their lavish generosity.

For I testify that according to their ability, and beyond their ability, they gave voluntarily, begging us insistently for the privilege of participating in the service for [the support of] the saints [in Jerusalem].

Not only [did they give materially] as we had hoped, but first they gave themselves to the Lord and to us [as His representatives] by the will of God [disregarding their personal interests and giving as much as they possibly could]."

Our love towards God's children will draw the Holy Spirit closer to us. It will guide us in our ways, preventing us from falling. Remember, you are not to love only the children of God, love everyone equally, do not show favoritism to any. When your children do wrong to others, do not cover them up, but reprimand them politely. Do not be afraid to admonish your children for the fear of losing members, but stand on the path of truth. By this you will gain respect for every and it will increase your stand with God for not abhorring evil. An upright man is a man God wants. Love to all renews our spirit, building us up as Overcomers.

The love of God brings wisdom. Our stand in God, non-compromise and renewal of the spirit will perfect our way, expose the devil and keep us from falling to the deceit of the devil. By His grace, we will always emerge as OVERCOMERS.

ABOUT THE AUTHOR

Bimpe Gold-Idowu is an evangelist and a teacher of the gospel. Blessed with prophetic gifts to minister effectively, build up ministers and discern spirit from one another.

A graduate of Divine Blessing Bible College and Seminary, Lagos, Nigeria, and the founder of The Seed Evangelical World Outreach, a ministry that deals in teaching the undiluted word of God, deliverance from the captivity of Satan, building up ministers for different denominations through spiritual impartation for the work of The Master in churches and reaching out to the less privileged, especially the orphanage.

Pastor Bimpe is married to Pastor Idowu Olaniyi Ezekiel. They both run the ministry and they have 3 lovely boys: Richard, David, and Ebenezer. Bimpe has several years of experience in both fiction and nonfiction literatures. She is into nonfiction religious books, Christian romance fiction, and science fiction genres.Her hobbies are cooking, reading, music, researching and soccer. Bimpe loves to hear from her readers.

To contact:
Website:
www.bimpegoldidowu.com
Facebook:
Bimpe Gold-Idowu
Twitter
@gold_bimpe
Goodreeds
Bimpe Gold-Idowu
Instagram:
@bookkindle_bimpegoldidowu
Email:
talktome@bimpegoldidowu.com,
bimpegoldidowu@gmail.com

Overcoming Deceit: Expository on the World of Lies and Illusions

Linktree:
https://linktr.ee/bimpegoldidowu
Tiktok:
@bimpegoldidowubooks

Printed in the USA
CPSIA information can be obtained
at www.ICGtesting.com
LVHW041628280723
753393LV00009B/1477

9 781088 132661